pretty

WINNER OF THE 2025 LAMBDA LITERARY AWARD FOR TRANSGENDER NONFICTION AND THE 2025 GLCA NEW WRITERS AWARD FOR CREATIVE NON-FICTION

"There is not one wasted paragraph or scene here. The language cradles but never, ever coddles. Some art just makes you thankful. I am so thankful." —Kiese Laymon, author of *Heavy*

"Every page of *Pretty* speaks to KB Brookins's longings and their willingness to be vulnerable in a world that threatens and erases. At the same time, a luminous thread of resistance runs through this fearless and engrossing narrative of becoming."

—Deesha Philyaw, author of *The Secret Lives of Church Ladies*

"The world is better because of KB Brookins. . . . From vibing to Frank Ocean's *Channel Orange* to praise dancing as a kid in church to their stunning and gorgeously rendered path to embracing their nonbinary identity, Brookins's stories will have you shedding a tear one second and holding your breath the next."

—Edgar Gomez, author of *Alligator Tears*

"A gorgeous memoir that, despite pain and rejection, insists on hope, forgiveness, and Black trans joy. 'You see gender, spinning and fusing into something freer?' Brookins asks. Thanks to their life-changing book, I do, I really do. There's no doubt about it: Brookins is the real deal."

—Marisa Crane, author of *I Keep My Exoskeletons to Myself*

"[*Pretty*] mixes poetry into the tenderly and skillfully narrated story of Brookins's life. . . . At its heart is a carefully sketched-out—and often devastating—portrait of what it means to be Black and trans-masculine in Texas, a state that continues to criminalize both of those identities."
—*Vogue*

"[A] powerful reminder of the undeniable force and importance of Black queer stories. . . . A moving and vulnerable foray into what it means to navigate and embody desirability/desire, tenderness, softness, love, and masculinity as a queer and trans person, Brookins's *Pretty* radiates honesty and authenticity. . . . [*Pretty*] is a ramifying reminder of the strength of hope, and an indicator of the revolutionary power that exists in our stories."
—GLAAD

"Brookins's writing thrives on well-observed juxtapositions. . . . Linguistically, Brookins pulls equally from playful internet slang and queer theory, often joining both syntaxes in the poems that punctuate each chapter. . . . Dazzling. . . . Brookins is a writer to watch."
—*Publishers Weekly*

"This book, above all, offers a potent narrative of learning to live authentically, no matter the circumstances and challenges. Brookins relays their experiences and opinions with candor. . . . An inspiring and deeply human work."
—*Kirkus Reviews*

"KB Brookins's debut memoir arrives when we need it most. . . . Striking. . . . *Pretty* offers far more than just pretty words—Brookins tells their side of the story as an act of resistance against those who would silence them."
—*BookPage*

KB Brookins

pretty

KB Brookins is a Black, queer, and trans writer and cultural worker from Texas. They are the author of *Freedom House* and *How to Identify Yourself with a Wound.* KB's poems and essays have been published by the Academy of American Poets, *Teen Vogue, Poetry,* Okayplayer, the Poetry Society of America, *Autostraddle,* and other venues. Their art installations have been featured by the Fine Arts Work Center and Prizer Arts and Letters. They have received fellowships from the National Endowment for the Arts, PEN America, Equality Texas, and others.

earthtokb.com

pretty

ALSO BY KB BROOKINS

Poetry

Freedom House

How to Identify Yourself with a Wound

Art Installations

Freedom House: An Exhibition

Y(our) Town

pretty

a memoir

KB Brookins

VINTAGE BOOKS
A DIVISION OF PENGUIN RANDOM HOUSE LLC
New York

FIRST VINTAGE BOOKS EDITION 2026

Published by Vintage Books, a division of Penguin Random House LLC, 1745 Broadway, New York, NY 10019. Originally published in hardcover in the United States by Alfred A. Knopf, a division of Penguin Random House LLC, New York, in 2024.

Vintage and colophon are registered trademarks of Penguin Random House LLC.

All interior photographs are from the author's collection.

The Library of Congress has cataloged the Knopf edition as follows:
Names: KB (Brookins), author.
Title: Pretty : a memoir / KB Brookins.
Description: First edition. | New York : Alfred A. Knopf, [2024].
Identifiers: LCCN 2023042976 | LCCN 2023042977 (ebook)
Subjects: LCSH: KB (Brookins) | African American transgender people—Texas. | African American men—Texas—Psychology. | Masculinity—Texas.
Classification: LCC HQ76.27.A37 K35 2024 (print) |
LCC HQ76.27.A37 (ebook) | DDC 305.38/896073—dc23
LC record available at https://lccn.loc.gov/2023042976
LC ebook record available at https://lccn.loc.gov/2023042977

Vintage Books Trade Paperback ISBN: 978-0-593-68488-7
eBook ISBN: 978-0-593-53715-2

Book design by Casey Hampton
Author photograph by Beowulf Sheehan

penguinrandomhouse.com | vintagebooks.com

Printed in the United States of America
$PrintCode

The authorized representative in the EU for product safety and compliance is Penguin Random House Ireland, Morrison Chambers, 32 Nassau Street, Dublin D02 YH68, Ireland, https://eu-contact.penguin.ie.

For Texas

& all my bois who didn't get to be boys

CONTENTS

two

three

four

AUTHOR'S NOTE

This is a memoir that I wish had existed when I started growing chest hair, and a patchy beard, and cut off all my chest tissue except the part that made fake nipples. This is the book I needed in high school, when I was getting ridiculed for being "gay." This is the book I need even still with my now-illustrious beard, as I blend in with men who have (or, more likely, haven't) dealt with their own monsters.

Before 2018, I identified as a Black lesbian from Texas. This was pre-COVID, pre-to-mid-Trump presidency, and during the times when everyone was catching Pokémon in random parking lots or doing the "Ur a Jerk" dance when we all had good knees. I was out here ridin' through the 6 (in this book, that means Stop 6, the side of town I grew up in in Fort Worth) with my woes, wearing pronouns and skinny jeans that didn't fit. I was in a body that felt fine except it didn't. Imagine me, a twelve-year-old in tights made out of 100 percent discomfort, seeing a stud* for the first time.

* Slang for "Black butch lesbian."

"Why is a boy here?!" a Black girl in my grade said to all the other seventh-grade girls in the gym. Slobber was still singed to the corners of our mouths. We didn't say it out loud but all wondered the same thing. The girl we were staring at in them oppressive-ass Spanx wasn't a boy. She was just lost in translation.*

I needed this book then, but I was too busy waiting in lunch lines for steroid-injected hot wings, eating three-for-a-dollar cookies so giant they covered half my face, and hiding in my sweaty, depressed body to inquire further than the common mistyped history in the falling-apart books you could only find in the 6. I didn't have an Amazon account then.

So this happened, first as just journal entries; walks around my now-Austin, Texas, block; conversations with my partner and other Black/trans/masculine beings; and bad, bad poems. Most names of people, plus some minor details, have been changed to preserve anonymity and fossilize this as my truth only. I include footnotes to make clear what I mean; some terms I use have multiple, or hard-to-find, meanings. I wrote this book on want and need to see Black AFAB trans literature. I wanted to share things about me and the un/templated masculinities I've seen over time from Black cishet men, Black gay men, Black trans men, and Black studs/butches/bois.† I wanted to figure out how Black AFAB trans people beam so bright like that, and remind us of how goddamn oppressive patriarchal masculinity is to everyone. I wanted my truth—just one that lives among the many of Black transmasculine people—to be centered in something other than death, and with the help of love,

* I go more into this story later in the book.

† When I say "boi" in this book, I mean transmasculine people, which includes Black butch lesbians, studs, dykes, trans men, and trans nonbinary people like me. Some transmascs use this term as a way to refer to the similar ways that we navigate and experience gender.

spit smeared on my screen, sleepless nights when my grades suffered more than they should have, and a hand-me-down laptop that's on its last leg, I think I did it, reader.

There are so many ways to experience Blackness and/or talk about the trans experience. Some of us are masculine, feminine, or something else entirely. Some of us are still figuring out the trench-coated brother with callused hands and Black & Mild stench, or the pants-sagging enby with a silk shirt and bad intentions; those are different templates of masculinity. I wanted to capture all those things, so I brought in my failures, my stories, my family, my critiques, my call-outs, my joy, and my jokes, in hopes that folks reading this might get what they need from it.

—KB Brookins

one

After Dionne Brand

The poet cloaks themselves in language
just to later arrive at your front door
The poet has been into the idea of mud lately—
where does it come from,

how do we track remnants of something that came
from an uppercased Something
and whine while wringing ourselves
dry? The poet has thoughts the size

of a mustard seed. Sits his ideas in our mud. Raises
up a child from the earth from whence it came,
stirs us up with the idea of tracking dirt. From dusk

to dawn, look. What do you see
in between mundane creases of shoes?
Can I breathe a penchant of insight into you

trouble-sized and ready to be loved?
The poet strips possibility bare
to count the lines on its hands.

Until I Wasn't

Before the Texas heat could cut through bodies like glass, there was a nighttime breeze. My mother felt a rumble in her belly that sent her hurling over a toilet seat—gunks of upchuck getting stuck in her hair. Sure, she'd gotten food poisoning or a bug that upset her stomach before, but this rumble was different. It stayed often. It felt unprecedented for her still-growing, seventeen-year-old body, so she hurried to get a pregnancy box from the pharmacy that is now an apartment complex.

She took round trips to the bathroom, each one more sobering than the other. After peeing on three different sticks, and spending minutes anxiously twiddling thumbs on her childhood bed, two red lines stood in for the inevitable: "pregnant." These lines were confirmation of what she already knew, but sometimes, someone or something else needs to say it. This was the end of her Black girlhood. This was the beginning of her sweet Black girl. Before she could count the days between the formation of her new self, a self forever molded by mothering, her first ultrasound appointment came. A nurse gelled her newly plump belly and pointed at a fatbacked monitor. Little lines went in and out of focus.

"It's a girl," the nurse said, softly. My mother smiled big, then nodded in silence. That was the first sentence of a book that describes my undoing. That was the first story someone else told for me.

At least, I'd like to think that's how it went. The truth is, I don't know much about my pre-life. My first thought was to start this book with some sob story about my childhood, something that made you want to tear up and keep flipping, but I don't remember much about that either. The learning how to walk, then run, then fail, then question myself—all of it is a blur, except moments that feel like scenes you hurry to forget after watching a scary movie. Unintentionally remembering little, I think, is the scariest feature one could have within their body/mind. I must confess: I spent many years making up stories about my 0–17 existence. I wanted my childhood to seem like the kind of thing that led me to the present, so I filled in blanks, and when friends inevitably recalled their childhoods in conversation, I told 50 percent fiction. I wanted the kind of memories that people bring up in quick quips. The truth is: when somebody says "childhood," my mind distills seventeen years down to several scenes I can count on two hands. Even then, my mind autocorrects to something else when I remember anything too painful. Half of those things I don't care to dwell on for longer than a few minutes (unless I'm in therapy). The rest of them, I guess, I will tell you.

Me and my bio-mom, circa 1996

The mind has a way of shielding the body from what it can't contain. Most minds don't have equal space for trauma and logic, so the latter takes a hit big enough to keep the other things working. So know that this origin story isn't the full one—who among us knows their life from embryo up to uttering their first cries, anyway?—but it is composed of the moments too interestingly gendered to pass up, starting with Barbie.

The aforementioned teenager who birthed me out of her womb was not ready to be a mother, so after two years of being raised by my granny, I was re-homed with loving, ill-prepared parents. The only folks I've ever called my parents are boomers; more religious, and much more rigid in their thinking, than a teen mom would be. My dad is a Texas-born-and-bred country boy, our extended family's handyman, and a deacon who spent forty of his able years fixing washing machines at Sears for a living. In his free time, he did an assortment of fishing, preaching, making everyone laugh, and making dishes out of anything he could kill (squirrels, deer, you name it). My mother is his equally religious, equally Texan right hand. Much more timid and quick-witted, she drove Fort Worth Independent School District buses for work and played the piano at church for some fifty-plus years before her memory started to decline. Neither of them has, to this day, lived outside of Fort Worth's Stop 6 neighborhood. Forty years my senior and empty nesters (both of their blood children were twenty-plus years older than me), they were more ready to parent, as my bio-mom and grandmother knew.

They loved me in a way that anybody who was raised in the '60s, who'd been given limited ideas of what love is, could. They loved me the way a child loves their favorite Barbie doll: enough to keep them alive, but not enough to keep them thriving. Enough to buy a child they chose to raise everything in their power but deprive them of what money couldn't buy. As for money, fixing appliances and driving buses didn't generate a lot of it. But man, were they rich in love for god and love for their immediate and extended families. So much so that at three, I had a box, bigger than me, full of toys.

Ever since I could walk, I undressed the Barbies my parents got for me at Walmart, Minyard, or Toys "R" Us naked to the manufactured bone. Those white, thin, blond, un-genitaled things were always splayed atop the covers of my childhood bed. While I was "playing with Barbies" age, my father loved to dress me up in these coordinated fits: dress, matching hat, matching shoes, and frilly socks. From 1997 to 2013, you would see no less than ten photos of me with dad-assembled drip and a tub of naked Barbies in multiple corners and walls of my childhood home. I took the clothes off every beige figure I could get my sticky hands on. I remember it feeling cathartic. Maybe I needed to see Barbie's boobies to understand what a body was. At least then, someone was naked, for no discernible reason, like me. If you need an image to ground you, picture a sweet Black girl in barrettes, dresses, stockings, and sparkly shoes undressing little plastic figures meant to signify white girls. Doing this was fun as fun could be.

In the world's mind—a world that never thought much of us Southern, working-class Black people—I may as well have been a plastic surface, naked until draped in gender. My dad dressed me like every little Black church girl in the '90s: crisp and nun-like. But who needs clothes when everyone has already defined you? I was a girl, so I played with Barbie dolls; secretly, I played with them in my own way. How odd: a toddler who already had secrets. Though I had no language for it, I knew that my Barbies should not have been naked. But on my terms, I made Barbie into the kind of girl—a frayed, nonsensical naked figure with no genitals and a smile—that I saw myself as. I put scissors to her hair and cut it multiple lengths, too. And then we played; me and naked Barbie played every day in Barbie's house, or on plastic-covered couches at my grandmother's house, or on tables and chairs and grass—every day until I moved on to other ways of processing my girlhood.

A false girlhood. A start button I didn't press.

I entered the institution of schooling at three years old. Due to my parents' demanding blue-collar jobs, they had to leave me somewhere from 6 a.m. to 5 p.m. They chose a small Christian Learning Center as the place that I would be, and every morning, me and all the other toddlers stood and pledged allegiance to two flags. I was mandated to know every word to the United States pledge like every other U.S. kid, but I also learned the Texas pledge—another indoctrination song—by the time I turned four. I learned how to pray to a god before I could understand the implications of a country. Then, we learned our numbers, colors, states of the allegedly United variety, and presidents, too. Girls were expected to wear "girl" clothes, answer in third person to she/her, play with Barbie dolls, and watch "girl" cartoons—the stuff adults defined as *normal.* A set of expectations and rigid structure for our small bodies and developing brains was good for us all, they thought (and still think). At three started a bevy of teachings I took a lifetime to unlearn, and I was a star student, known to be the first one at daycare and last one to leave. Gender started as an implicit unsaid, a thing I didn't know how to question.

One of my favorite pictures of myself was taken in that same Christian Learning Center on picture day in 1998. Every year, the center brought some photographer to set up a backdrop and take portraits—ideally of a kid smiling at the camera—and charge parents some meager amount to have a new picture on their fridge or in their wallets. The picture taken of me that day shows me in a black and red dress.

My arms were fluffed up with stuffy cotton fabric. An auntie of mine did my hair that morning, and the barrettes were so tight that I held my head in awkward positions for the rest of the day to alleviate the pain, including during picture day. My navy praise-dance necktie, the only girl-coded necktie in the Family Dollar we went to three days before, was used to accent my dress, a boring plaid-patterned mess. Cause we were a Christian center, all the girls had to pose with their hands cupped into each other (don't ask me how this makes sense). I gave an empty stare to the camera—my big light brown eyes dilated, looking down the barrel of the lackluster lens. My hands were as awkward-looking as possible, clearly indicating some kind of discomfort. I remember a teacher yelling, "Smile!" seconds before the flick of the flash. Instead, I fossilized my feelings. It is the only childhood picture of me that I like.

Daycare picture day, 1998

I wish I could remember what I was thinking. There's something about the honesty of it that's always haunted me. My mother hung it up in the living room, then the dining room; these days, it sits in my parents' house behind a guitar that never gets played. I look blank, as if to say, "I'm only here so I don't get fined."* It felt good, being treated like a little Black girl, until it didn't.

The first time I knew I was a girl, I was five years removed from the womb, in the backseat of my mama's green 1997 Lincoln Town Car—the same car she drove to work, church, and back home from the bus barn where she worked long hours for little, but enough to feed and clothe me when coupled with Dad's dollars made at Sears. By the time my mama pulled up to the dirt road of the little blue building, a repurposed house that I went to daycare in, I was ready to go home and play in a place where I didn't have to share toys or think too much about my body. I had "only child syndrome," I guess. Cause of Mama's hectic bus barn schedule, I was almost always the last kid to get picked up.

"Woof!" I said as I alley-ooped myself into the car. I sighed as if I had just gotten off the same shift as my mama. "I'm tired." She chuckled and then patted her forehead with a hand towel she kept on her for hot days on the bus.

"You ain't lyin'," she said back, in an actually tired voice. "What did you learn at school today?"

"Same ole, same ole. We went over our names, numbers, and the presidents of America." In 2000, Texas institutions taught you presidents after names and numbers.

"Oh yeah? Name me some of 'em," she said, looking at me like I was lying through my teeth.

"George Washington, John Adams, Thomas Jefferson . . . ," I

* I'm riffing this quote from Marshawn Lynch's 2015 Super Bowl interview.

listed, with my stubbly fingers counting to three. I was unsure which colonizer came next, and my mama looked at me, eager to hear my larger-than-life self say another white man's name.

"James Madison!" I said, finally remembering. Mama looked so proud of me as we got a block away from the place I called home from 6 a.m. to 5 p.m. every weekday.

Back then, I didn't know much about America or its henchmen. I knew my name, that I loved my parents, and that I lived in this big ole state named Texas. I knew my mama worked at the bus barn and my dad fixed these big things called washing machines. He also drove a big blue truck with S-E-A-R-S on the side of it. I knew my granny took care of kids, so I couldn't always be over there. I knew my mama's name, my dad's name, and the name of four dead white guys. I know my parents did as much as possible to make me happy. When my mama picked me up from daycare, everything was all grits and gravy. That was at least until I got to the "inquisitive" age.

As I was talking to my mother, my legs were plopped open so wide that I could part a red sea. Nobody told me how to sit (cause why would they?), so this was my default mode in any chair. By the age of five, the year 2000, this started to become a problem.

"Close your legs, girl. There are men around." At this time in my life, anytime adults said something I didn't understand, I answered with a "why."

"Why, Mama?" I said, in a voice two octaves away from hers. Mama's smile lessened to a resting face. The "men" in question were my father. Why would I need to care about that?

"You don't wanna know. Now pull your skirt down and sit right." My dad always had me in these knee-length skirts, as if every day was picture day, and Mama had my hair all prim and proper. By the end of daycare days, the skirts were often wrinkled and my ponytails were two inches away from where they originally were. My mama went to work every day in a burgundy FORT WORTH ISD shirt and a floor-length skirt. Usually, cause she needed ankle support to push buses through the city, she wore Walmart-brand shoes to match.

"Why, Mama?" I said again, in the same voice and sitting closer to her face.

"I mean you need to do what I say and sit back while I'm driving. You hear me?" she said, this time sternly. Her resting face disintegrated into a frown. Since I didn't wanna get my butt smacked, and I'd learned to not question Mama once I heard her tone of voice change, I sat back and played with the zipper on my backpack. Getting inquisitive got me in trouble, but the occasional answer felt worth it.

I would go on to hear that same phrase—"there are men around"—at least a handful of times every week.

"Put on pants, there are men around!"

"Put on a shirt, there are men around!"

The frequency of those admonitions only got more aggressive when I grew breasts and hips. All these statements, these almost-pieces of advice, came without an answer to my original inquisitive questioning. At five years old—the year before I left daycare to start first grade—I got sexually assaulted by three teenage American boys my "play auntie" mothered. Even after then, I didn't get an explanation. Why did I, already at five years old, need to change how I exist in my body for men?

At my first elementary school, a Christian private school with loose regulation and questionable morals, I had to wear red and black dresses. Picture a fabric that grates your skin and has absolutely no ounce of drip. They were made of stiff shit you could only find at one overpriced, faraway store. They were coupled with the ugliest, most uncomfortable black church shoes that made playing at recess so uncomfortable, I often broke them in defiance. We also had to wear white undershirts, which anyone with good sense knows doesn't work for children. My mother's dates with detergent and Shout stain remover quadrupled while I attended this school. But nonetheless, my parents' high school friends ran it, and I'm 90 percent sure they gave them a discount, so I had to go. I don't remember much from this time, but I could never forget the first day of school.

After my parents dropped me off at the school that looked like multiple repurposed homes, I remember looking out into the crowd of my new peers. My Barbie backpack dangled from my back as I saw kids sitting on a basketball court in huddles, talking among people they seemed to have known their whole minuscule lives. I saw tiny heads jutting back in laughter and adults speaking in their huddles on the sidelines. My stupid heart kept me worried about going to a new school so much that I hadn't gotten any sleep the night before, and this scene just about confirmed every concern I had. Though I stiffened every bone in my body to fight it, the waterworks were stronger than my balled-up fists. Tears formed in my eyes, and I pushed out all my body's anxiety-water till my dark brown face turned red.

On the surface, it was cause I had nowhere to sit. Every person—tomboys, prissy girls, and booger-flicking boys—had a huddle that it looked like they belonged to; even the kids who played Yu-Gi-Oh! found their kith, happily dealing their cards among each other. When I looked onto that court full of squeaky church shoes and stressed young adults, I saw no huddle that fit my personality (which was naked Barbies, burps loud enough to laugh at, and a bedazzled CD player with gospel mixes made by my piano-playing mother). For the first time, it occurred to me that I was *different.*

Sure, at six, people's personalities are malleable. Girls liking Lil Bow Wow and then switching over to Lil Romeo was an almost weekly occurrence. But at that moment, I had no clue who my people were or could be. In under five minutes, I scanned hundreds of kids' faces for a hint of hesitation like mine, or closed-off body language like mine, or things being pulled out of their backpacks that resembled something I'd like; nothing familiar appeared. I couldn't find my people on that basketball court; I couldn't find them among the teachers or admins either. Everybody seemed to be mid-conversation, mid-laugh, completely comfortable (or doing a great job at feigning comfortability) but me. Instead of trying to understand why I was crying, my body did what any body does when it's introduced to something unexplainable: it started to excavate. Instead of relying on my six-year-old grasp of English and emotional intelligence, I did the same thing I did on daycare picture day and held it somewhat together. I forced myself to get un-pink. This was a decades-long habit formed at three: bottling shit up.

It is the law of the land, to *belong* with at least one person everywhere you go. If you don't, you'll be ridiculed. To this day, I get the most stares when I dare to do things alone. At six, my "somewhere" was with my Barbies and parents. At three, it was on my blue sleepy mat or, when it was still appropriate, playing by myself. At my elementary school, a school dripping with the kind of Christianity that cuts queer and trans kids out like weeds, I had to find a corner of something inside of me that was at least like one other kid at the school. When others looked up while I was having my meltdown, I had to quickly hide my pink.

To be a *girl* at this point, then, was to be dainty and happy and believable, though if *girl* was X, and *boy* was Y, I was already the illest infinity sign. But I had to be un-me, so I was. Until I wasn't.

A year into attending elementary school, I fit in just enough. Girls talked to me only when they were paired with me in classes, and boys loved to pick me for their kickball teams. I could knock that red rubber ball out of the park with my feet. To this day, despite my parents putting me in damn near every sport throughout my childhood, kickball is the only sport I'm any good at. Every good kickball team needs a kicker that gets automatic points on the board, so I was picked first every time. Me and those happy, many-shades-of-Black boys ran base to base with nothing trailing us but the wind every time I could talk myself into being social enough to play kickball. On days when I was too anxious to play, let alone exist, I'd just play in the sand, or on the merry-go-round, or inside with the adults by myself, ignoring the eyes of judgment burning the back of my neck. It's not that I was a sore thumb, but surely I was a hurt limb amongst the *normal* girls at school. Regardless, it didn't matter when I could kick a ball next to Black boys with smiles large enough to stretch twice around the sun. I sometimes smiled just cause they did. Their joy, which eventually turned into mine, pumped through my quickly beating heart as I ran as fast as I could from base to base.

During one kickball game in the spring of 2002, James Kendrick decided that it was his duty to stop me from winning. At eight years old, he often was the ball-roller that called the shots. If he told a pack of smelly elementary school boys to move in one direction, they all did. James excelled in kickball, soccer, and basketball—the only sports one could play during an hour of recess in a midsize backyard-length field. Everyone wanted him on their team first, except when we played kickball.

For kickball, everyone wanted me first, and naturally, cause of the way we've set up the world, he took offense.

"You're pretty good for a girl," he'd often say while he ironically negotiated to get picked for whatever team I was on. On this day, he intentionally played against me. He made it a goal, his goal, to catch me slippin' today, and win.

Some urban legend claims that boys flirt by being mean, and that's true, kind of. When you're a loner kid like I was, you learn to listen and see more than you speak and believe. So I watched James navigate his own journey into gender. He walked with his head as high as an eight-year-old could make it; he prided himself on being into sports, Transformers, and "man stuff." He stayed away from girls since they had "cooties," and he only ever talked about his interests and his dad, clearly his model for how to live life.

"My dad has two motorcycles," he said as he was playing *Crash Bandicoot* on his blue Game Boy. All the boys listened in awe, wishing they had a dad that cool. Despite us being at a private school, and all the churchy-ass adults around us trying to act like we were getting an education *so much better* than public school, the families of kids at our school still had public school issues. Homelessness. Food insecurity. Addiction. At this point, I didn't know to care at all about whether I had a dad, though I know my dad loved me fiercely. All the boys without dads at home already knew to hold it in their hearts: the envy they felt for James's dad, the brokenness they felt at what they thought they were missing.

James closed his Game Boy's head, and continued to talk about how cool his dad's motorcycles looked. To me, they looked and sounded like metal death machines. He was a boy all boys at school could cling to. He often smirked as he walked past me with all the boys that followed him on the kickball court.

We started our game, and I played as I always did. My kick was forceful, precise; I kicked it out of the court every time. Due to James's tactful cheating, our teams were tied. He'd roll the ball when people weren't paying attention, call "out" even if a ball bounced out of someone's hands—you know, "man stuff." Recess was close to being over, and everyone was getting tired of playing.

"Could we just call it a tie?" I practically begged.

"Never!" he yelled, then rolled the ball quickly to my feet. I kicked, with the little energy I had left, and this time, it didn't go out of the park. Instead, the ball wiggled through the branches of an old oak tree. Every boy on his team surrounded it, ready to catch my unfortunate kick. Once the ball rolled out of the tree's large branches, it fell perfectly into James's hand. You would've thought he won a prize, or got the biggest monster car for Christmas, with the way he grinned, so pleased with himself for holding us back from resting before class.

"You're out!" he yelled. I looked at him with no discernible expression. I didn't care even half as much as he did about kickball (or anything else), but he wanted a stronger reaction. He then threw the ball at my chest to force that out of me.

His throw briefly took my breath away. Think five pounds of rubber, barreled into a seven-year-old's flat chest. A feeling bubbled up in me that I'd never felt before. It was scary, I thought, to be this upset at anything. Enraged, I kicked the ball into his chest, causing him to quickly plop onto the ground, dirt covering his body like a cloud. He cried until his dark brown face turned pink, which elicited a concerned look from all the players, and other kids, and adults who stopped in their tracks, wondering what had just happened.

It was the kick heard around the school . . . all two thousand feet of it. Once the adults shook off their shock, they came over and helped him get up. He pointed at me with tears still rolling down his face.

"That manly girl did it!" He winced. Everyone looked at me, known to be the weird quiet kid, in confusion. How could anything I did cause James to cry like this? Other boys, especially the older ones, chuckled at his misfortune. Older girls found him a bit less interesting, and whispered unpleasantries to each other. He scanned the audience, then said the searing phrase while pointing again:

"That manly girl did it!"

When his dad came and picked him up later that day, his teacher, the only teacher for all the second graders at the school, explained what had happened that day. He sustained no physical injuries—just the emotional injury of embarrassment. His dad looked him up and down, his eyes still red from crying on and off. Without a second thought, his dad barked:

"What I tell you 'bout that punk shit?" I stopped playing in dirt, compelled to just listen. "You gotta toughen up!" he said to James. James nodded his bowed-down head.

Despite my actions, I got no reprimand, mostly because of adults' erasure of my existence. If anything, James's hatred was the consequence that kept on giving. For the rest of elementary school, James decided that I was his archenemy. Nary a day went by without a snide comment or dirty look received from James Kendrick. Little boys are a lot of things; *mean* must be on the top of the list. This boy was one of many reasons I hated going to that school; even now, driving by those blue buildings when I visit my hometown awakens something in my nervous system. This man-in-training made three years of my life feel like hell. It was as if I'd shat in his Lunchables, or as if he'd left the school on a stretcher, the way he sustained his bullying and rage.

But maybe I did something worse than that. Maybe I exposed that he, an eight-year-old Black boy, one of the many Black boys who used to sport a big smile, wasn't the man everyone started to act like he was.

Contending with My Want (To Be Normal)

In all my childhood dreams, I was a boy.
Meaning in all my dreams I had 3C hair,

yellow skin, phenotypically Black features like
full lips and a crisp hairline only a Black barber

can bless you with. I was a cis boy.
In this version, the most the desirable by those I wanted

to desire me—Black girls of any shade and body type,
Black boys with long torsos and too much shame

to waste on footballs and bad dreams. I had clothes.
Mannerisms and idioms like *damn, girl* and *my dude*

and a face that is wanted and easy. A non-twisted walk.
Teeth straight as my deepest desires

(to be wild enough in my want), straight like
lines where the razor hits my forehead and sideburns.

I had a beard and a girlfriend or two. Everything
a beloved human in Black heaven, which is desire,

could want. I had a working definition of family.
He had a family that wanted him home.

Lost

This day in church, I stood next to Mama. I was a praise dancer, prancing into small church aisles singing "Silver & Gold" by Kirk Franklin. We all wore stockings and headbands; I wore multicolored barrettes and a cotton white shirt with a collar. My shirt was tucked into a dress, plaid-patterned and bigly loved amongst the usher women at church. I was the smallest ~~boy~~ praise dancer in church, and everyone loved me so much that I always inherited aunties and cousins. There are many pictures of me in that church smiling, crawling, always being the center of someone's attention. My clothes, and church activities, and life, came from choices made by somebody else. But I was five, heavenly innocent in the year 2000, unassuming and in adoration of a new, indubious world.

While Mama talked with adults after service, I played tag with the other church kids. I said "You're it!" when inevitably picked as the runner and tagging someone else. I was told by kids and adults alike to "slow down" and "play softer," often. This day, out of the many Sundays we spent in this big, redbrick church, Mama called me over to her and my aunt Fey (aka Mama's friend from church). They were joined by a boy whose dick was in my mouth earlier that week who looked angry about something. He looked something like a pit bull who knows they peed in a corner inside.

"You know when you did that thing for me earlier this week? That wasn't supposed to happen," he said, weighed down by his got-caught guilt. Two adults decided that now, in the middle of a game of tag, outside of a church building after we heard the preacher preach about submitting ourselves to Christ (whatever that means), was the time to address the sexual violence that was happening under everyone's noses. *What am I supposed to say,* I thought to myself. For months, three boys violated me unchecked; this happened every time my aunt Fey was supposed to babysit me, and instead left me alone with her three boys and daughter, which was often.

"I'll throw you in the air and make you laugh all day long; just do this for us," the teenage assaulters said on nights I stayed with them.

I don't remember much of this time in my life, but I do remember that the boy at the church that day was the only one that got caught. I do remember their beards, how age sat differently on them than me, their insistence that doing this, putting their genitals in my mouth, would be fun, that they would throw me in the air like the little girl I was after I did a teenage task for them. I remember every Sunday, me in stockings and them in tall tees, my body unscathed, their clothes laced with weed that darkened their lips, the dark house made even darker with secrets and nobody around to raise these brothers, my questions, my body, my reluctant yes. I remember my lack of thinness from birth, comments about my weight from these teenage boys within minutes of meeting them. I remember being a woman before I could ever be a girl. I was a girl in the imagination of others and nowhere else.

Of course, there were families in the church that knew about them. The delinquent teenage boys that my aunt Fey raised, the boys with thirty-two teeth and insatiable hunger for ~~animals~~ girls in lower food chains with shorter legs to run. I listened to the gossiping about them.

"They need to get baptized," another aunt said.

"They are just being boys," her husband, a grown man who excused their violence, countered.

The only language I had for responding to betrayal, violence, and insincere apologies at five years young was "okay." I whispered this, unable to make eye contact with a boy who willfully manipulated me, and he nodded his head in silence. I knew something about what they made me do was wrong; anything that you won't do when your mama's home is wrong, usually. I kept playing until we went home. We switched churches and never talked about this incident again.

At the age of five I started to go missing. I was the lovable ~~girl~~ caricature of a human my parents wished and wished for. Surprisingly, I've grown to not blame my aunt. How could she have known that her sons would do such a thing to another child? How could she have known that a boy, even when you are a single mother, even when there is no man around to taint the ways they think about women, even when you drag them to church every Sunday, will learn what it means to be a man through the exploitation of women and girls? It would be too simple to hold contempt for a woman who, like all women I grew up around, was trying to survive. To this day, I'm not sure I'm even mad at the boys. The adults that let them terrorize girls unchecked, and the systems that reward patriarchal violence, and the mentalities that let church grounds continuously be the grounds where sexual assault blooms, and the silence, the loud, terrorizing silence that left me with questions for decades, are the real culprits. But there is no accountability to bestow on ideas, just stories. So I'm telling this to you for the girl I was, and the girls that unfortunately feel me, too.

Every day I wake up and a Black ~~boy girl~~ goner has gone missing or uncared for. Or erased by communities meant to protect them. Every day I wake up and even more people like me, little ~~boy girl~~ miracles, are uncounted to begin with. I create the other side inside of me with every injection I fill with a syringe and shoot into a muscle.

You see that light flickering in the distance? You see men, repenting and skipping out on their well-known sins? You see the thinness of that woman's grief? You see the love nested in that ~~man's~~ person's beard? You see gender, spinning and fusing into something freer? You see the tree, connecting roots underground with their siblings in the middle of a storm? You see that present left outside a dark room?

I am no longer lost. Can you find me here?

The Game of Letting Things Go

If the feeling was liquid, what would it be?
Water, seeing how I've gone 28 years without washing away my sins
Oil, since everything that feels fair & just in this world slips away
from me
Blood, since it's on my hands every time I try to shave
Mercury, since being me is deadly
Milk, since I can't digest the fact that I'm in a hell that I can't
escape
Jell-O, since I'm still, but only when violently visible
Broth, in case you want to set fire to me for fun
Syrup, sticky with happy lies that keep me alive

What container would it be in?
An AM radio station
A cup
A cone
A can
A case for the Texas flag flown at the governor's mansion
A coffin
A gray-blue cup used for canvas paint
A camera lens
A jar of worms escaping
A car
A brothel
A wife

Where are you gonna throw that liquid?
In the face of every transphobe in this state
On the neighbor's lawn
On the gentrifier who is complacent with the ghost of this town's sins' lawn
On the doorstep of every person with Black blood on their hands
On a cop's doorstep
On a politician's doorstep
On you if you don't ~~listen~~ get me out of this non-consensual hellscape
Inside me then outside while the earth cracks open & swallows us whole to build a new world

There Are Miracles and Blessings for Me

This was the song my cousin sang. My cousin, a ten-year-old skinny Black girl who sported luscious hair and frilly pink dresses. DeeDee stretched her pipsqueak voice over any organ or keyboard riff at the churches our family drug us to. She was the first kid in my generation to be assigned a solo.

And justifiably so. DeeDee was a normal girl, happy to be indoctrinated into our family name. Often, her rendition of Gaye Arbuckle's "Miracles and Blessings" wasn't on the church service's agenda; she was just called up to sing it at the drop of a hat. She did it with no pushback. Cause of this, and more adult-made tensions, I was predisposed to eventually hating my cousin. Though two years younger than me, DeeDee was the first girl I was forced to look up to.

Lord, I thank you for this day
that was not promised to me

For sixty years, my family has maintained two gospel singing troupes made up of our 100+-deep bloodline. We're from Fort Worth, Texas, and known as the large, animated family that sings and plays instruments for god. Our last name is something like legendary; if my mother talked to someone for more than ten minutes at our local Fiesta, somehow she found out that me and this stranger were cousins, or that the stranger knew and loved someone in our family. DeeDee was happy to go to the schools our aunts and uncles went to, or get stopped at the mall by someone who knew our mother's mother when her last name was something else. Though many people over many generations went off to college or the military, no one in my family stayed away from the Fort Worth metroplex for more than four years. All these regular occurrences, and all these years of presence in our big-but-small town, were the legacy DeeDee and I inherited. Only one of us inherited it willingly.

Our family is overwhelmingly composed of women. Our matriarch, Big Mama, had four girls and three boys. Those kids had kids that were mostly girls. Then those kids' kids had kids like me and DeeDee, millennials expected to be girls. Cause I've never been anything akin to *girl,* the women in our family had lots of questions for me.

"Why don't you close your legs?" or "Why do you dress that way?" were regular asks, and then when I got older, "Why don't you come around?" They didn't ask these questions of DeeDee. She wore dresses and skirts and played with Barbie dolls. She closed her legs when she sat, and didn't act "fast" (a term wrongfully attributed to me cause I didn't care to change my whole personality around men). She could sing, and didn't groan when we had the third church service of the day, like me. She didn't question the Bible, or why girls couldn't sit or stand a certain way, like me. She was the light within, if you let elders tell it, inevitable darkness—the promise that our family wouldn't erupt in disarray once older folk passed on. DeeDee was proof that tradition, when you don't question it, prevails and pushes forward.

For me, keeping up appearances for strangers in pews feels more backward than anything else. Deeming every girl that doesn't perform high femininity as a "curse," and deeming femininity you don't like as "Jezebel behavior," surely is a U-turn straight to hell. But to our family, it was just a part of being a god-fearing woman raising god-fearing (read: *normal*) girls. Elder women in my family were mean, rude, and nosy as hell. But like any kid, I had a groundwater-deep need to blend in with my family. I already wasn't fitting in at school, so the least god could do was give me a family I could feel safe with. But, just like a family member, god gave what I wanted—praise and pristine social status—to DeeDee instead.

Lord, I thank you for my health and strength
And saving me one day

Members of our family founded and frequented Baptist churches, so it was regular to see and hear people respond to what was happening in services. People onstage and behind the pulpit could say or do anything and people would clap, yell "Preach, preacher!," scream "Amen, brother!," and wave their hands, signaling to everyone that the spirit was moving them. People would run around the church, dance from their seats to the middle of aisles; some women would stand and sit so often throughout services, I wondered why they bothered wearing heels, or shoes at all. So, since almost everyone seemed to "let the Lord use them," when I stood I thought no one would care. Everyone around me reacted.

DeeDee was singing "Miracles and Blessings" just like she sang last week, and I decided to stand up. I saw the demeanor of people who treated me like a lost cause completely one-eighty. An old woman stared at me like I'd conjured a ghost, and the old geezer next to her said something to the effect of "Sweet Jesus." An auntie on the other side of the aisle said, "Alright now" and started clapping. It was as if they thought me using my legs to stand signified something grander. Everyone's reaction told me they had never thought I would come around to it.

And then I realized: DeeDee was singing during the altar call. Of course, they thought I was going to the front to confess my "sins" or something. My only sin was being butch, full of questions, and alive. If I'd had the balls, I would've cussed everybody out right then and there, but instead, I stood, letting the attention of people who think themselves Christ wash all over me.

When I think about the things I want
Not the things god knows I really need

At twelve years old, I already identified as an apathetic churchgoer. I often sat in the back pews unless an elder forced me to be closer. I stayed on my white, gas station, Virgin Mobile phone texting friends throughout entire services until my auntie ushers started to swipe it. Then I started bringing my Game Boy or my CD player to pass time; the hours spent sitting on uncomfortable pews felt excruciating. "Only here cause my parents drug me here" was practically written on my face, or at least in the mean mugs I gave all the nosy ushers and too-good relatives. For hours out of my weeks, I wished that I was anywhere else: a music video, a video game. I would've even chose being at school, *middle* school, over church. That's how much blues it gave me.

But it wasn't my fault. I'd already associated church with negative vibes, since all adults at church did was nag me or ask my parents if I was gay. I didn't quite know what "gay" was yet, but I knew that I was suspected to be it (my aunts couldn't whisper that well). That's why, to me, it was comical that, at family reunions after I went to college, folks had the audacity to ask me, "Why don't you come to church anymore?," as if anybody would choose to be around people delusional enough to think that their hypocritical asses were going to heaven. As if anybody would want to frequent a building built on judgment and bigotry, though they tell themselves they've made "god's house." God should've tore that shit down brick by brick. God should've evicted every damn body who was more worried about my queerness than doing close readings of the book they used to condemn me. If they did that, they'd know that gossiping is a sin. If they did that, then I wouldn't have had to run so quickly away from them.

There are miracles and blessings for me

I don't know why I stood up in church that day. Maybe I finally saw the words in a new light. Maybe it's cause "Lord, I thank you for this day" felt real, considering that I didn't want to live at all during most of them. Maybe cause by twelve, I had already begun binge-eating, skipping showers, and letting depression take me, so the fact that I had any health and strength left was a miracle in and of itself. Maybe cause a higher power kept saving me, kept pulling me off the ledge of my mind, so I must've been here for something, right? Little did I know it was to write. Maybe it's cause the things I wanted were the exact things I needed: Love from my family. An eye that met mine that didn't see me as a joke, or a nuisance, or a problem for god to solve. Maybe it's cause I'd already felt miracles.

As soon as I left my parents' house for college, though I went to college in the same town as my family, I left my churchgoing days behind me. In the past ten years, I've maybe been at a church five times: to pick up a girl, to drop a boy off, to meet a they/them cause we couldn't find a place to bone that we wouldn't get busted at, to watch my godson be christened, and to read a poem at a church that was nice enough to make me their artist in residence. I've grown up to learn that #NotAllChurches are bad, but have decided against religion altogether. There *has* to be a higher power; there's too much in the world that is extraordinary and unexplainable for there not to be. But I'm fine with not knowing what it is, and firm in my belief that a relationship with my spirit doesn't start and end at whether or not I go to church.

This is the reality of many church girls who were forced to be girls against their will. Even DeeDee, who still goes to church every Sunday, and whom I hated for a while but eventually forgave for all the shit she regurgitated from people who were supposed to love us. I've grown enough to be exposed to real love—the kind that doesn't force you to be a gender you're not. We put pressure on kids and then adults to live up to ideals some power-hungry religious leaders made up, willfully misinterpreting passages in the Bible. I've read the Bible front to back twice; nowhere in there did I find that women should be modest, judgmental, and date men and only men (no matter how much people try to twist and turn those two passages in Leviticus). Instead of worrying about upholding tradition, I wish that my family was interested in questioning it—*What does family mean to us? What have we done to make some people run away? Can we love each other better in the future?* These are the questions I wish they'd ask, but I can't make anyone fall out of love with their own delusion.

DeeDee and Gayle Arbuckle were right: there are miracles and blessings for me. I had to sprint to them, and completely fall out of the good graces of people who were my blood in order to get to them. The biggest miracle of my life is making it to a place where I'm not ashamed of the harmless truth of my being: I am not a girl, and my love doesn't depend on a lover's gender identity. Through the noise of multiple generations of beautifully talented, wrong-headed people, I got there. It is a miracle that I did. My blessings are the opportunities I've had to save my own life; the friends I've made that see me, all of me, and want to be in my life as long as life lets them; the feeling I get after I write all this down and know that those mornings (and afternoons, and nights) facing a pulpit didn't break me.

Once I tuned out all the noise from the adults around me after I stood up, I just closed my eyes; pictured my happy place, which at the time was my bedroom. I knew that I would make it through that church service, and the next one, until I could make miracles on my own. DeeDee sang the second verse like she'd really been through something, seen something, felt something like deliverance; I just swayed and swayed along to the music. Still, my eyes were closed, and for the first time, I pictured myself as an adult. I saw a life that wasn't just tomorrow. If this was "spirit work," it was working on me. By the time she finished the song, my arms were up and tears were streaming down my cheeks. I didn't know then why I was crying. When I look back over that day, and the many days after it, I see a kid lost in the shadows of a toxic church culture I felt like I'd never escape; maybe I was crying cause seeing a healthy adult in my mind meant I would escape it. In any event, I clapped along with everyone else and sat down.

When DeeDee came to my pew to sit down next to me, she asked the inevitable question.

"Hey, I saw you from the stage crying. Are you good?"

"Yeah," I said, softly. And I was, eventually. We sat through the rest of church, went to our respective homes, and glided through our childhoods being complete opposites. In the end, it didn't matter at all.

Good School

Them kids on the westside don't have a better school.
They just ain't have 2 cops & lie detectors greeting them

at the entrance of their day. They had textbooks
without ripples, they parents had legacy jobs

& they legacy was one our people earned but they people
spend & write in wills. They walk without the haunting

of boys who didn't make it out the schoolyard &
smoke shit that comes in dust instead of dried-up trees.

Just because they catch a high & we catch cases
for non-criminal offenses, just because their girls

get to be seen as girls & not something to be fixed into
a tool for control, just because queers

code-switched till we could Usain Bolt
away forever, they ain't better than us.

Why you never ask why we *bad*?
Why we fight each other until the edge of death

comes to sing one of us home? Why you never ask
'bout our hearts, what makes them sign this life

away in blood & angst? Until you do,
don't tell me nothin 'bout no good school.

On My Hometown

I'm from a city most call Dallas, but Texans know is Fort Worth. Though relatively unknown outside of our region, my city is the hot commodity of North Texas. Every Black kid within inches of our infamous, segregated city wanted to be from Funkytown, where the boys brawl over invisible lines in dirt, where the girls stuff weed and Victoria's Secret from the Mexican mall (now called La Gran Plaza) under their skirts.

I say "segregated" cause segregation never really ceased in Fort Worth. Way back, the east side was Black, Southside was Latine/x, and the north and west sides (with the exception of Black-ass Como) were white as the snow that fell once every two years. Gradually, Latine/x folk migrated east and took up 2 to 10 percent of the population, but since the '50s, these demographics have stayed the same. Maybe I met two white folk from birth to seventeen. My neck of the woods/my little side of the east was Stop 6, home of the Dunbar Wildcats and a 40 percent poverty rate. On both family sides, my adopted family's and bio-mother's, two-to-three generations of my folks have lived, loved, and lost within this four-mile radius. I'm one of not many in my family who have moved more than a hundred miles away.

As is the case in most Black neighborhoods, we had our issues. Gang activity, poverty-related crime, and domestic violence were what landed us on many Worst Neighborhoods to Live in North Texas lists. Despite stats put together by folk who never saw us, I made great memories on my lil blocks of Blackness—swinging on front porches, and getting single cigarettes at the corner store without an ID. So many things about me are cooked into the streets of

Stop 6; so many lies I told to stay out late smoking with friends at local parks. So many selves I had to hide from and only let free in the dark. Stop 6 was my little slice of Black heaven.

It was also a congregation. Every church and mom-and-pop shop was Black. Every holiday felt like Juneteenth—lines were long as Lake Arlington for BBQ plates on days we had off. We had bash after bash at Lake Arlington. I long for and miss this unintentional Blackness most when I'm in the white ~~power~~ tower of academia, and while I'm trying to find consistent Black friends in my ever-gentrifying now-home of Austin, Texas. Yes, Stop 6 had its issues, but we also had our magic.

In 2008, I—just like every other Black kid with parents that worked late and a granny that was happy if we were doing anything quietly—was watching too much *106 & Park* and *Rap City.* I also snuck and watched *BET: Uncut,* Comedy Central, and MTV. Though none of those shows were set in my place, this state stolen from Mexico that we call Texas, every kid around me wanted to be a caricature of those young adults on TV.

I probably grew up around ten Lil Bow Wow wannabes. 50leven girls wanted to be Ciara. Probably six or seven boys with tattoos and a budding smoking problem were Chamillionaire in their head. All the popular girl cliques did their best to let me know that I was "weird" while sporting Cherish-style lip gloss and bangles. I was more "Weightless" by All Time Low, "Heartless" by Kanye West—more Kid Cudi's "Day 'N' Night." I did my best at genderless sadness.

On any given day of middle school, I wore skinny jeans, rhinestone belts, and an aura that told you "I'm emo," if nothing else. I remember laughing cause some boy said "titties" randomly in math class, but no other instance of me laughing around my peers comes to mind. I didn't speak unless spoken to; I kept my head down, swiveled my iPod Nano to the highest volume, and knew that if I showed anything more than this, any more of me, I would be drowning in even more bullying about my weight and a sexuality I never even claimed than I already was.

I was in eighth grade: the time in grade school best known for identity crises. I remember getting dropped off at school with my signature Barbie backpack (at the time, every adolescent wanted to sport a cartoon bag), and was walking toward the one friend I'd managed to make in middle school. She was smiling, happy to see me after sixteen hours (which was years in middle-school time), when a popular girl crashed into my shoulder like a wave, almost knocking me off my feet.

"Get out of the way, you bitch, you freak, you dyke!" she said, looking directly into my eyes. A comma isn't enough to explain the pauses she took after every sinister insult. It was like she was pausing to conjure the meanest thing one could think of in her moment of unnecessary rage. It's as if I gave this girl a carton of piss instead of the breakfast milk she was carrying (which wasn't spilled or harmed in our clash).

I stood frozen in place. At thirteen, I didn't know what a dyke was, but I knew it was something bad. Everyone paused mid-conversation with whomever they were yelling to look at me and her, a real-time freeze frame of some untamed thing they hoped sprung into a fight. Without understanding of the last insult hurled at me, I was exposed, raw, naked with embarrassment.

"Damn, she called you a dyke and walked off," my friend whispered, as if that helped the situation.

"You gon' let her talk to you like that?" a stranger asked, within earshot of others wondering the same thing.

"Nah. Nah, I'm not," I said with a gradually rising voice, as if I really had a choice in the matter. I'd spent seventh grade being everyone's punching bag, so I was determined to stand up for myself this new school year. Ill-equipped, I was ready to fight for my right to not be a dyke.

The summer after this incident, Fort Worth was in the national news for the first time in my life. In a homophobic, Stonewall-esque tirade, both the Texas Alcoholic Beverage Commission (TABC) and the Fort Worth police raided the Rainbow Lounge, the oldest (and only) gay bar in town, which had just rebranded from its old name ("the 651"). It was a nightmare for every in and out queer person in the city.

Multiple folks were arrested for public intoxication (though they were inside of a bar), and one person received severe brain and head injuries after being slammed into the ground. The only rationale cops offered up was that patrons were "coming on to them." Folks who were detained were later released without arrest. A terrible coincidence: this incident took place on the fortieth anniversary of the Stonewall riots. The club burned down in a fire eight years later.

My reaction to this news was mostly internal. Sure, it's clear that this place was targeted for being a gay bar, but even in my little Black heaven, people were putting folks in a kind of hell for being any kind of queer. Around this time, the first lady of a church my father preached at and mother played the piano at (for free, mind you) decided that all women should wear skirts. The rationale was something like "women should be more womanly"—a clear dig at me, since every other woman in the thirty-person congregation drank the Kool-Aid of traditional womanhood. Three years before this, I received the worst whooping of my life for getting caught in sexual activity (which later I realized was an instance of someone assaulting me) with a teen. I was constantly badgered by adults and peers about the small amount of hair growing under my nose and my always-baggy jeans. Already in my adolescent life, anything anyone around me thought resembled queerness was quickly punished. This news just confirmed, on a local scale, what I already knew: *Queer isn't something I can be out loud while within the limits of this city.*

In response to this hate crime, local queer adults started organizing. A Facebook group titled Rainbow Lounge Raid had some fifteen thousand members. A Dallas-based group held a vigil to honor the victims; a day after the raid, about two hundred activists staged a protest at the Tarrant County Courthouse, and other protests followed. The mayor of Fort Worth refused to apologize for the raid, and police did and said nothing. Many years later, I read in *Captive Genders: Trans Embodiment and the Prison Industrial Complex* that the community's response was just a vigil. There is constant revision of this story and its significance to Fort Worth queers. This is unfortunately typical: the erasure of the Southern resistance within LGBTQIA+ movements.

Back then, there was no support group in Fort Worth for LGBTQIA+ youth. Or adults, for that matter; only bars, which now seemed unsafe to attend. In Stop 6, I had the Black church, my school, my relatives, and my friends—all of whom held anti-LGBTQIA+ sentiments. All my friends were kids who also didn't fit in, and most were confined to school-hours friendships. Not at school, nor at home, nor at family functions where I was surrounded by people I thought loved me, did I feel *normal.* Since the time in my life where I started to show bits and pieces of my personality, or at least my middle-school obsessions, everyone started treating me differently. It's like all love—or at least all love that worked for me—stopped when I started to be *me.*

When I think of this time in my life, I think of how the offense

I took to the word "dyke" was influenced by my surroundings and nothing else. When I think of my response at the instant of being called a dyke, knowing at that moment the only thing it could be was some kind of queer, I think of everything around me telling me to be something else.

And so I was. For three more years, I defended myself with my fists or my lips against constant whisperings that I was gay. I dated boys (often older than me than they should've been) in order to prove it. I quieted my desire for girl classmates and their pretty hair, cute outfits, and beautiful Black skin cause I couldn't live *like that.* "The Bible is against it," the church said. And my parents, friends, and skin. Despite my desperate efforts, the network of whispers at school, at home, and in my family only got bigger as I got older.

No longer obsessed with the aesthetics of an early-2000s white boy, I started wearing every layer I could and calling it "fashion from the future." On any given day of ninth grade, I'd wear an Aéropostale shirt, rhinestone belts, 3D glasses with the lenses pushed out, a plaid long-sleeve, artificially distressed skinny jeans from Goodwill, high-top Vans or multicolored Converse, and jewelry. Occasionally, a graphic tee would be in the mix. I wore lots and lots of i <3 boobies bracelets, cubic zirconia earrings, and fake-shell necklaces. It was the future, though (aka: androgynous nonsense). My self-esteem was so low, but my dressing game was on a kite.

"You have your own look and I like that about you" was an often-dished-out remark I got from creepy senior boys. I sported a ponytail and rock star attire—this was the only thing I could wear that my parents accepted as *girl* attire, though it was on the brink of *boy.* Still, it wasn't enough proximity to *girl,* so peers and family members alike gossiped—everywhere except to my face.

"She cross-dressing now?" I overheard while sleeping at an auntie's house. My cousin DeeDee and her mom—my older cousin—

snickered while whispering about me, as if there wasn't a sliver of chance I would wake up and hear their vitriol. I couldn't run away from their house, and my mama was still two hours away, at a church playing the piano for a congregation that would rather me be normal. All I did was fall asleep, and that somehow gave them license to do this. If I was "cross-dressing," I was doing a bad job at it, since a mix of "women's" and "men's" clothes could easily be found in my closet, and boys were the only things I wrote about in all my journals.

I could tell you that I didn't have queer thoughts, but I'd be lying through my teeth. I went back to sleep, hoping something sweet in a dream could heal that newly created wound.

Anybody within my life that was cross-dressing—or anything close to it, like me—was whispered about. And worse, they could be the subject of a sermon at the sin-filled churches my parents and relatives frequented. What I was doing with myself—being myself—was not okay to them, just like children out of wedlock, though they were much more forgiving about that. To them, gays and lesbians (the LGBTQIA+ acronym hadn't caught on yet) spoke too much about "rights" when they should've been getting "right" with god. It was volatile, to be anything but small enough to fit in their holy boxes.

Boxes weren't big anywhere near this place stolen from Mexico that we call Texas, the place that I grew up in. None of the boxes were big enough to fit me. "Texas, why don't you want me here?" was a sentence written continuously in my journal and heart.

By tenth grade, I was so stressed about this self-denial (along with the regular woes of being a teen) that I lost seventy pounds in two years. Though compliments were plenty, I wasn't eating; only worrying and quieting. Around this time, I also started going to a new church. After years of ridicule from adults who should've known better than to gossip about a teenager, I told my mother that if I was to stay a Christian, I had to do it elsewhere. She understood. I started going to a church with more kids, hopeful that this would alleviate the pain of constant stares and accusations from adults.

And there she sat, my first girlfriend, in the back row of the kid section.

We met within my first week of being at the church, then she snuck me an invite to her apartment complex in Arlington. I was a fine little thing, still dressing androgynously, and she was a femme four years my senior who couldn't resist the Sapphic aura I emitted no matter the suppression. Her eyes were soft. Her lips, even softer. She wasn't easy on the eyes, but I loved the attention. Craved it. It felt better than any romantic experience I'd had up until then.

During services, we would look at each other and smirk. It was our secret, being friends and then some. I wish I could say that this was our "happily ever after," but many things stood in the way of us being. When I started to come over too much, homegirl's mother asked if she was gay.

"No," she said adamantly. Anytime her mother was home when we hung out, her mother was short with me, visibly uncomfortable, and suspicious of our supposed friendship. We kept on as long as we could with our puppy love on the low. Nobody at church besides her brother knew, and we planned to keep it that way forever.

That was until the pastor of this supposedly progressive church took my girl's mother to the side, and said lines I'll never forget:

"An usher is telling me that [deadname] is looking at your daughter. Be careful," he whispered. The same words were uttered to me days later from my girl.

All of a sudden, I felt negative about that church and any church in general. Were people really *looking* at me? Was everyone so uncomfortable with my presence that they had to spend time monitoring my every move like that, watching where my eyes went, and how my face contorted when I looked at my beloved? Of course, they didn't suspect anything of her. Of course, I was the only one that was the talk of adults at the church. When the questions in my head became too loud, much to my parents' discomfort, I elected to stay home on Sundays.

Not a day goes by in my now-adult life when I don't see religious indoctrination—especially of Christianity, the religion baked into my seventeen-and-down existence—and cringe. There are still Black churches out there not letting their queer folks be honest. Queerness still impacts how I navigate space.

The trips I don't take to states and countries hostile to LGBTQIA+ people; the clubs I don't enter; the times I don't display my chest via mesh shirt (even though I love to show off this body I paid racks on whenever I can)—from the time I emerged from a womb in Fort Worth to the now-days I spend in "liberal" Austin, there is a forbidden display of my bodymind. Texas legislation and the comments section of any well-known LGBTQIA+ person's social media proves it.

The history of queer life has been depoliticized in order to fit into mainstream LGBTQIA+ orgs' assimilationist, capitalist dreams. Cause of the lives I've lived, I know there is no meeting in the middle with people who want to oppress me. There is no meeting to be had between me and folk who try to blame their violence and contempt toward LGBTQIA+ people on religious books badly translated and written before Black people were seen as human. The Bible was written before capitalism and a lot of other present-day problems, yet folk hold on to it as if anything meant to be right is meant to be right in perpetuity.

Black existence is already synonymous with worry—so close you can taste it, or far away till it's summoned like the moon—that you won't be given the benefit of a doubt. That someone not Black will doubt your humanness today and create another network left with nothing but less life. If we're lucky (I mean viral), our mourning families get a lump sum that doesn't amount to what we've lost once someone decides to take a Black life from us, and our lives turn into fodder for non-Black liberal social media content. Another hashtag and delete. Despite #BlackExcellence, #BlackJoy, #BlackMenFrolicking—all things invented by Black folk to combat narratives of Black abjection—worry lives in us as much as blood. We do everything in our power to be happy while worry rises and falls in us. There is no Black existence that lives in these states that wrongly call themselves "United" without the worry that our displeasure with being treated poorly will be read as anger. It's true: Black folks have come far in the realm of rights, but not far enough for all people and systems to love us, or at least tolerate us enough to stop denying us life. On every corner of every street, the possibility that a cop will stop me and decide I don't need to breathe exists. Then *boom:* another lineage of Black people left with less. Black existence is worry that you will be cheated from life.

Queer existence is watching the best of Congress and the richest of our nonprofit sector say that marriage and more carceral penalties will stop you from bleeding out on the sidewalk. Gay marriage didn't stop a club shooter's dad from being happy he isn't gay. "Don't say, don't tell" repeals didn't stop the homophobic shooter or cop from getting a battery in his back enough to brutalize you. Queer existence is waiting for another Pulse Club, another shooter getting a gun for his fifteenth birthday; even in "progressive" cities—ones queer folk move to so we can be more of ourselves—aren't 100 percent safe. We know this, the fact that we can't *be* unless the pride parade is ousted from our veins. We can dissociate, crowd ourselves with those who *get it* in clubs and centers, but Twitter User Number Whatever and pundits on Fox News still remind us that we are unholy. Joe Biden will still tell his Republican colleagues that our rights can be negotiated out of existence. Religious fundamentalism—which still forcibly runs the U.S.A.—will legislate us out of existence, or tell clerks and priests they can deny our already-fickle rights. The streets—which are home to many LGBTQIA+ youth—still hurl epithets at us. In childhood, I was told I was unfitting for the home of god, as if god themselves would approve of their followers condemning people. False prophets still tell queer people we must be less of ourselves to get into heaven.

And all of this won't stop the doctor's office from calling you the wrong name. It won't stop trans people from not being *real* in some eyes—usually when you're thin and white—and being *what's wrong with America* in others. Transness is wanting fewer people to miss, and instead, getting pronoun pins. It's wanting forcibly elected leaders and @ names hiding behind cartoon avatars to stop worrying about what genitalia is in your pants. It's wanting many Americans to stop making your existence a one-up, a ploy to get the votes of losers who are too drunk on ignorance to learn anything about trans existence. Transness is forty-nine lawmakers in forty-nine states wanting your carnage and spirit dead cause you dared to be yourself, is being wrongfully accused of "mutilating children," is knowing bigots and those who've fallen prey to bigot propaganda want you rotting in the ground they'll eventually mull over to build condos. You are a condo's base, the cold earth of misrepresented bodies that gets told its worth by government bodies, if you are trans.

Try existing with all three. Try knowing that your state, and your slice of Black heaven, wants you dead and forgotten like all the other Black queer and trans people who didn't survive to get out like me.

Every day that I wake up able to live the life I do, I know that I'm walking uncharted territory: the newly self-acquired land of my body. I'm breaking into expressions and ways of being intentionally axed from history. I'm being everything I am as openly as I can cause I want to do something better than just survive. I owe it to the ancestors that insisted on my living.

Still, there are many things out of my control. My childhood, the ways that I must interact with the places I call home (for now), and my family understanding me fully among them. But as long as I'm breathing, I'm challenging the deeply ingrained colonialist norms of gender and sexuality. Four hundred–plus years after the original American mess-making, and white supremacy is still fragmenting me from my people. I rebuke that, in the name of whatever god exists.

What could my hometown, Texas, and the world look like if Black queer and trans people didn't fear every day that we will perish? What if those fears, mandated by law and those who claim to be our god-fearing loved ones, didn't exist? What god has told folk it's okay, encouraged even, to treat other people so terribly? What god has told homophobes, transphobes, racists, and Bible-thumpers to limit centuries of love?

When will queer and trans people be seen as citizens in this place stolen from Mexico that we call Texas? Will many Texas politicians ever gain a conscience? Aren't queer and trans people—people who simply have a different experience of gender/sexuality than our cishet counterparts—deserving of comfort, safety, and promise like everyone else? When will trans people be cleared of the longstanding lie that we are enemies of women and girls?

Through all this terror, I'm 90 percent sure there will never be a Texas without me. A handful of people can make this state livable if they fell out of love with bigotry and greed. Though we are a long way from it, and a long way from queer and trans people feeling fully safe in any place in the U.S.A., it isn't out of reach. I want the next generation of queer and trans kids to be celebrated, not made to feel abnormal. And they will be when we are honest about our problems, and artists, policymakers, cultural workers, and people in all cities work with us to solve it.

I would love to exist in this place, and be Black, queer, and trans without it being an issue. I'd love a Texas where I can go to the doctor, and pee, and play sports like every cishet does without the added layers of sorrow. I'd love to see my family, be close to my family, get apologies from my family; I'd love to live in a Stop 6 where I can say "there will never be a Texas without trans people" and all the beautiful Black faces that populate the area, my area, believe me. How would my love—for other beings, for my hometown and state—be if we could truly be "out"?

These are the questions that keep me writing and chasing the past. Everything I am is of god.

two

How to Identify Yourself with a Wound (2018)

I am a woman only under certain conditions. When
needing a hand moving furniture. On ladies' night
at the poorly lit bar when the bouncer touches
my lower back. He says "Right this way, ma'am"
and I swallow a cringe along with the complimentary
whiskey and coke. When tits protrude through my mostly-
stretched binder. When a man decides to grab my friend.
I step in and say "Back the fuck up"; the laugh he bellies
reminds me I was a woman then. When the bass
in my voice is reduced to a crack, a chest, some child-
bearing hips. When Beyoncé says "ladies" in "Me, Myself and I."
The last sip before we leave tells me maybe
I can deal with being every kind of woman. Who am I kidding:
I've only ever been a question. Laugh? Womb? Wound? Sure.
I am mistaken for a woman only under certain conditions.

Who Am I Kidding: I've Only Ever Been a Question

I am a woman only under certain conditions.

And that's true, kind of. For the short time that I was a woman, I was a sliver of something other than myself. Before trauma brought me into a ~~terror~~ consciousness about intercommunal violence, I understood myself as a human. Not an example, or a mistake, or a gender even. Before any binaries entered my thoughts, before the phrase "there are men around" was ever uttered to me/toward me/in spite of me, I was a person in between dimensions. A being trying to figure out how I could be seen as human.

I guess I was a woman then.

Creating your own conclusions about what it means to be a person is something no child should have to do. No adults—not my mother, father, or the parents of those boys who first violated my bodily autonomy—asked me what I wanted. There were no apologies from my people, or from the rape culture we normalize; just passivity. I see discussion among strangers on Twitter about the role victimized women could~~n't~~ have played in their own demise. I wanted to be a child. While I was a child, I wasn't a child. To be a woman is to be asked to do somebody else's work plus your own, thread somebody else's fabric. Being a woman is contributing to the fabric of a society that breaks you. It never was my choice.

When / needing a hand moving furniture.

At nine years old, I didn't have an agenda. Only after-school dates with the television, flipping through channels that came with my granny's DirecTV, hoping to catch *106 & Park* before it went off. Every weekday, I rushed to my granny's van, parked right outside the school at 4 p.m. just to catch ten videos with quips from AJ and Free in between. Sometimes, they even had guests.

Once, I rewound one, two, three times just to see the introduction and full three minutes and fifty-six seconds of the music video for "Oh" by Ciara and Ludacris. They both—especially Ciara—had me glued to the screen, thinking and feeling things I'd never thought and felt before. When I first saw this video, I probably wasn't any bigger than Cece, the little girl Ciara spoke to in the first seven seconds of it. Like me, she was focused on watching every move of the "Oh" video. I wore Twinbead Bubble Ball Ponytail Elastics in my head like Cece too—especially the classic white ones. Every weeknight, while the song was in its promotional run, me, a little Black being by the eventual-name of KB, sat ready—my hair, loosely still in the shape of what my mother made it look like in the morning. My clothes, once white and now a dusted off-white—slouching on my body while I gawk at Ciara and Ludacris's world, brought to my granny's TV by Sho'Nuff recordings.

Ciara's face at 0:11 is what first got me. On what looks like a black and bronze wall connected to a long alleyway, she leans her bronze body and looks directly at the camera. In my mind, she was softly telling me, "Hey." A couple more shots of her flicker until it gets to the main setting of the video, one including a close-up of her lips. At the time, everyone wanted their lip gloss to be poppin'—accentuating their glossy skin tone in pink. I'd like to think the videographers knew what they were doing with this shot. At the time of this video, Ciara was the peak Black woman.

What I mean by "peak" is complicated. Two thousand four was a time when, similar but different to now, everyone cared about looks. Then, the "peak" Black woman was slim, at least a little light-skinned, and rocked a straight weave/glossy lips/thin eyebrows/bushy eyelashes combo. Ciara had all this, and she wasn't afraid to show you in every clip of every video. Often, her shirts stopped at her bra, giving needed face time to her impressively lean stomach. The "peak" Black woman wasn't muscular, either; just slim, supple, hairless, like Ciara.

The video goes on. She reemerges in an orange and blue crop top, jeans that are cuffed above her ankles, and tennis shoes; she dances along to her song with a crowd of Black folks backing her up. It oozes Southern, these scenes, specifically pulling from a car show in Atlanta, this one specifically put on for Atlanta's then-princess, Ciara. Notably, many of her dance moves require that she moves her hips, directing our attention to her washboard abs and slim-thick composition. It's no wonder a whole city was backing her. She was the standard, the thing to be seen amongst flashy cars and equally talented dancers. She was the peak—our dancing, yellow-brown queen. It's no wonder why the rumors started.

Around the same time as her rise in Black fame, someone started saying she was born male and, specifically, was intersex. For the time, this was considered salacious, and—if true—would have made her predominantly Black fans lose all respect and admiration for her. Cause haters and the drama they peddle exist in every timeline, this rumor spread quickly. The day after my daily ritual of watching "Oh" on loop, I overheard a conversation in the hallway between Black boys that sounded like this:

"You know Ciara is intersex?"

"Yeah bro. That shit gay!"

"Shole is."

In an instant, the woman I secretly desired was seen as a bamboozler, a gender illusion. Black women felt cheated, and Black men felt grossed out. All of a sudden, people pointed to proof in her cheeks and abs, and how the camera hit her slender face. Then more lies compounded—"she talked about it on *Oprah,*" they said. Then it was "she told her parents she wanted to be a girl at five and they let her grow her hair out," then "she was born with both parts and then had surgery to become all female," then, the ultimate kicker, "she's a lesbian." All this shit was made up by adults and kids out of thin air. An iterative lie, a bout of jealousy that turned into a nationwide panic about the genitalia of Ciara, a nineteen-year-old who was one of the few embodiments of the peak Black woman.

That was the earliest message I got—loud and clear from other Black people—that veering away from the gender you were socialized as would strip you of all desirability and favor. At nine (the age I was when "Oh" came out), I was always shaping up to be a problem for the strict rules of femininity, since I wanted my hair in a low ponytail and loathed the ultra-feminized skirts my elementary school made us wear. I didn't have half the feminine energy Ciara had, yet Black pop culture stripped her of all that when they caught whiff of a baseless rumor.

It got so bad that Ciara addressed the rumor on *106 & Park,* saying, simply, "Come on, now." When host AJ heard the word "intersex" come out of Ciara's mouth—which took a while to even get to, due to her clear discomfort with saying the word—his brow rose. She also addressed the "lesbian" rumor, saying this:

"The bigger and better things get for you, the more people try to bring you down." Down. Being a lesbian was, to 2004 Black pop culture, people bringing her down. Free agreed. Everyone in the crowd clapped. Down.

The hardest thing to accept is that I can't be mad at anyone in this scenario. Not Ciara, Free, AJ, nor the discomfort coloring the room as they talked into shotty mics on a multicolored couch. I can't be mad at Black people (most of the time) for being homophobic;

it's one of the many isms and phobias that are baked into the conditioning we've continuously gotten since coming to these states. What I mean is, Black Americans were forced onto this land in 1619 and had to be taught to be misogynistic, which is a derivative of homophobia; to detest men for being "feminine" and detest women for not being men is to twist misogyny into anti-queerness. We were forced to learn Christianity, but not in the way any god intended.

I know now that we were indoctrinated into Christo-fascism so slavers could justify their sinful, godless actions. There is no god that tells his followers to hate queer people. There is no god that would give you scripture saying "[god] created humankind in his image" then tell you to hate trans people for modifying their bodies, but be okay with cishets getting various gender-affirming body modifications. That is all bigotry. That is what was and continues to be forced on the Black American psyche. The hardest thing to accept is that although queerphobia is not our inheritance, it is our responsibility to rid ourselves of it. It is, and continues to be, our job to rid ourselves of the white supremacist, patriarchal, cishet thinking that keeps us wanting to be the oppressor instead of wanting to be ourselves. We are our only hope for survival and salvation.

On ladies' night / at the poorly lit bar when the bouncer touches / my lower back.

If being a girl was a graded assignment, I failed with D's and F's. At ten years old, when every girl around me was beginning to woo the Lil Romeos of the world, I wanted so badly to play ball with the boys. Cause I was born with two left feet, and too much anxiety (among many other misfortunes), I couldn't play ball well either. The boys thought of me as a boy—good at kickball and picking dirt from under picnic tables with them. Not good enough to hold hands with, and surely off-limits for any "hide and go get it."

I was fine with this. Sure, I wanted a boy to like me, cause that's what I was told to want. Sure, I felt something when the hands of a beautiful Black boy brushed up against mine, but I knew they would think nothing of it. I was a boy, or almost-boy, to them. They were interested in the Ciara types. Though those didn't exist among my ten-year-old counterparts, the potential of a girl growing up to be a Ciara flickered behind a Black boy's eyes.

They didn't see that future me. I didn't see it for myself. Queerness came to me like the kickball at every recess—red rubber beauty, and at the perfect pace. I knocked it out of the park, and I caught hell for it. I couldn't escape the box of womanness, but at least I was good at something else.

He says "Right this way, ma'am" / and I swallow a cringe along with the complimentary / whiskey and coke.

Also, at ten, I met a thirteen-year-old named Lyriq. Every adult told me, "Come hang out with the girls for once," so I did just that with her, hoping to get homophobic hands off my back.

Lyriq taught me the boys I should like, the porn I should watch; she showed me examples of pictures I should take in her blurry-ass mirror deep in her dungeon of a bedroom we called "the girls' room." She taught me how to message boys back when they inevitably hit me up after her yassification of my MySpace page. It was her space, actually, but I thought this was just how girls made friends.

"A ho is a girl who got all the boys in a *bad* way," she said multiple days and nights after. I'd be Lyriq, somebody else, then be deserving of the type of love where a boy will feel you up. At least I thought that's what the goal was; I had nothing to compare it to. I had no other friendships with girls to help me know that this one was growing to be inappropriate. One night, after church ended and I went back to her place, she stuck her hands under my pants while we were taking our post-church nap. I jerked up immediately, screaming: "What are you doing?" She laughed.

"I'm doing what I always do with my friends. Chill and lay down."

Again, I had nothing to compare it to. I guessed friends sometimes touched pussies.

She did this for what felt like hours while my body lay stiffer than a pillar of salt. *Does this mean I'm going to hell? Does this count as one of the sins preachers harp on during sermons; does "a man lying with a man"* work the other way around?* She couldn't care less that I wasn't participating—her only goal was to explore. What exactly, I'm unsure, but her fingers seemed to explore everything. I closed my eyes, sure that it would be over soon; then I felt a wetness that made my eyes bulge.

"What the fuck," I said. She also taught me how to curse. I looked below the covers and there she was, face-deep in an area of my body I'd never even touched myself.

"It's just head," she said. "I promise, it feels good after a while." I hoped it did.

Things went on like this for years, despite my comfort or consent.

When tits protrude through my mostly- / stretched binder.

Fat. FAT. Fat. It sounds staccato and immediately stings a negative emotion. I've never been small; always "more than enough meat on

* A remix of Leviticus 20:13, a passage of the Bible bigots often use to justify their homophobia.

them bones," in the words of mean men and boys. I first heard the term "fat" on TV shows like *Moesha.* Then I heard it all the time, in elementary school, said to me like a verbal middle finger. I then heard it from my dad, and the boys that abused me, and Lyriq, and every day of my childhood I can remember.

"You know, if you were a couple pounds smaller, you'd get all the boys," one of the boys that abused me said. That's what the boys saw when they saw me—the promise of something to publicly lust after—if I were smaller, more femme, less me. I hated that so much that I would cry.

Nappy-haired, brown-skinned, and fat. I wasn't given girlhood or fragility. Most Black girls that were ever fat Black girls in places other than their homes, or even in their homes, are owed a million apologies. I didn't want to be fat, or a girl, or alive.

When a man decides to grab my friend.

The only moments in womanhood that I think of fondly are the ones when I could lean on somebody. The empty nicety of a man holding the door open for you can be a saving grace after a day of feeling unfit for anything *woman.* I thank the sexist gestures that assume a woman is too dainty or unfit to be moving furniture herself. I stumbled into womanhood after a checkered girlhood wanting to be everything deemed "normal." And pretty. The placenta wasn't washed away before I was given womanly chores: *Be clothed. Be cautious of strangers. Don't leave your legs open.* I learned to live every day as if a man could come up to you and buy/bury/bungee jump into your body. To him, none of your input is needed. If I could have bought my way out, I would've gone broke trying to; I promise you.

Black women are meant to be delicate, yet strong enough to

clean up a man's mess. The least I could do was benefit from empty gestures like someone offering to move my furniture. In other words, the meal was created, cooked, and served. It was eaten without me and still, I was expected to praise the crumbs.

"Man" is an obstacle "woman" is expected to overcome. We stick together cause we have to; "we all we got," women and girls would say to me. Even around the one girl I'd come to befriend, I wasn't safe, was violated, was treated like a science experiment. So where did that leave me? What did I do to make myself a target for any gender to bruise?

I step in and say "Back the fuck up";

A doctor said "it's a girl," and I fought for that to be right. Even when I knew it was wrong, I tried my hardest to be *girl* in ways I saw others be *girl.* Telling an eagle it's supposed to be a pigeon doesn't change the fact that it's a fucking eagle. It doesn't help when that eagle's a baby, expected to sprout new plumage so soon. I was never the opposite of femininity, just not its equal synonym; to everyone, that meant I was wrong.

the laugh he bellies / reminds me I was a woman then.

No matter how hard ~~Lyriq my mother BET every auntie~~ everybody tried to save me from me, I couldn't help it. I am who I am. In an anti-Black, anti-fat world, that meant, for years, that I felt undesirable.

When the bass / in my voice is reduced to a crack, a chest, some child- / bearing hips.

In eleventh grade, I decided to lean into my butchness. From the moment I started wearing chinos, it seemed as if every girl in the district caught a whiff of my gay from miles away—the desire for me immediately went up. With the exception of girls hell-bent on getting a fit, basketball-type stud from the suburbs, I was swimming in a sea of femmes, so deep and plentiful. I was that nigga unless I was in the "real" world—you know, the one where cishet and queer-repressed folks still didn't like my being.

Though queerness finally gave me desire, I still compromised myself; I still had to deal with false chin-checks.

"You know you still a girl, right?"

"I'll fuck you till you straight."

"You ain't gay. You just haven't met the right guy."

Every ignorant sentiment was "you still in that body" in more tasteless, violent words. With one surgery and fifty needles, I shut them all the hell up.

When Beyoncé says "ladies" in "Me, Myself and I."

Abnormal women look like trans men vibing to Beyoncé. They look like enbies moving their hips to what they wish they could forget. They look like me, a being with many scars, raising my glass to the sky in a dirty club, telling myself that everything I've done to get here was worth it.

The last sip before we leave tells me maybe / I can deal with being every kind of woman.

The cool thing about being trans and white is you get to be anything you want. Wear makeup, get a mustache (if it's in your genetic blessings), be "roadkill from the cisheteropatriarchy" for Halloween. If you're Black and trans, you get to struggle. Condragulations,* you get to be misunderstood by anything not Black, *and* not trans.

The ball is in your court. Wear makeup, go have sex with strangers. The cool thing about being trans in general is that everyone thinks you chose this life. Most things that come with "this life"— the bigots, the misinformed, the assaulters, and the greedy—is someone else's choice.

Who am I kidding: / I've only ever been a question.

The sliver of time that I don't have to be a man or a woman, the sliver of time I can breathe with my circle, the sliver of time that I'm not juxtaposed with one restroom or assumption, are the best few hours of my life. Everything outside of it is the worst few hours of my life. Being me is knowing this.

Laugh? Womb? Wound? Sure.

What is so funny about my existence? Is it that it's what's left after shame? Is it that I'm an amalgamation of resilience I didn't want? Tell me, please. I'm on my last set of trauma.

Once, when my soul was up to the brim with ache, the kind that was ten years in the making, I walked down during the altar call at church. It was the second church I stopped attending cause me being gay was an issue; they thought they knew me cause they followed a false god. I walked down, already teary-eyed, hoping somebody, anybody with their hands stretched out to god, could cure me of this disease that was tearing me away from my family. This

* A term popularized by RuPaul Andre Charles.

queerness. This thing that made me unpretty. The pastor's wife met me there. She held my hands and said, "Repeat after me:

"I. AM. A WOMAN."

I said, "I. AM. A WOMAN."

"Once more, I. AM. A WOMAN."

"I. AM. A WOMAN."

"One more time, I. AM. A WOMAN."

I hollered, "I. AM. A WOMAN." Tears fell from my eyes like they had been there, waiting for me to unleash them. She yelled as if the Holy Ghost was in the room, finally bringing me home. I went to bed, hoping that my taste for women—what I actually went down there to cure—would be gone.

It wasn't. And I wasn't a woman.

I am mistaken for a woman only under certain conditions.

I've always been me: fat, Black, queer, trans, and pretty. I deserve a world where I don't have to be resilient.

We skip school to listen

to Jill Scott as we spin
on a merry-go-round.
We say *I'll miss you*
& that's the mushiest
we got, for now. We make
MLK community center our home
away from gays too afraid
to be honest. We look up
at the muggy sky, humming riffs
of *A Long Walk.* We walk back
to school, where we drop into
days that queer like midnight clouds.
We think *I love you,*
instead say *let's go back*
before the hall monitors trip.
We trip on melted sidewalks
that make grooves of their own
in the shape of our feet.
We skip school to swing
jump & stumble into
our new love

Channel Orange Taught Me

In summer 2012, I was a Black masculine lesbian going into my senior year of high school. My two other out masc friends were girl-obsessed. When I say they were girl-obsessed, I mean I haven't fucked with one of them since 2013 cause she chose to hang out with a girl instead of coming to my graduation. She tried to justify it: "Bro. B, that's my girl. You understand." GIRL. OBSESSED. We were kings.

Like many high schoolers with home and family issues, I was with my friends more than anybody else. We linked during passing periods, in Kik group chats, and after school. We ate hot chips and smoked weed together at the corner store up the street. We bitch-shopped (as we called it then, forgive me) at every mall in our area and fantasized about meeting our own Beyoncé together. I didn't have anybody else to talk to about the things that kept me up at night—girls and what to do with my body—so I stayed with my kings in the thick of the worst summer-leading-into-fall of my life.

I spent that entire summer conditioning (read: *being hazed*) for a drum major position. All through high school, being in the Wildcat Marching Band at Dunbar High School was my thing. It got me all my friends, and it was *the* Black band in the Fort Worth, Texas, public school district. If you know anything about Black bands, you know that we practiced at least forty hours for every fifteen-minute halftime show and showed OUT—synchronized line dances and drum routines galore—for two hours every football game. The days were brutal, and the two hours before and after band practice that I had to stay back and do more—to prove I was tough enough, mature enough, *man* enough to be trying out for drum major—

were even worse. To be a drum major was to be top of the food chain. To be front and center of every show—of every formation that the band, dancers, cheerleaders, and audience members looked toward as those stadium lights flashed down. For that recognition, me and three other drum major candidates did high kicks until our legs begged us to stop. We did burpees, ran laps, and blew whistles until we couldn't bear the pain—all just to prove to our directors, two grown-ass Black men who relived their golden years of being in Grambling University's band by hazing teenagers, that our suffering was for something greater. I remember doing push-ups as the Texas sun simmered our skin at least two shades darker, yelling with every up-and-down motion:

> *"I like it / I love it / I want more of it / make it hurt / drum majors / make it hurt."*

Looking back, I see now that my respectable-but-still-in-the-hood-ass school was not ready for a fat, Black, masculine lesbian to be head honcho top of the food chain of all high school arts endeavors. But this was my first ballsy endeavor in my life, and I was determined to get one of three hot spots in the Wildcat band. I must've shed something like twenty pounds trying to get my mile down to ten minutes. I learned every complicated dance move—spins, splits, and air-humping motions included—and became good enough at working out that I could encourage band members who were ready to quit on exercises. I hadn't cared to keep up with everyone else less than two months earlier, but my body got stronger in a way I'd never experienced. I simultaneously became the kind of leader I'd never seen—no-nonsense enough to demand that everybody do better, and tenderhearted enough to tell the other fat kids to gulp eight big glasses of water each day. I told them to flick off anyone making

Me and my friend Devaun, fooling around in the band hall around the time I auditioned for drum major, circa 2012

Me (middle-left) on snare drum, playing in the Dunbar Wildcat Band, circa 2011

Me, smoking with my kings, who were smart enough to stay out of the frame, circa 2012

cheap shots at their expense. In three months, I went from clowning on the drumline to giving pep talks to the outcasts of an already outcasted group of kids. If I wasn't the best dancer, surely I was the best leader by a long shot.

And then, something happened.

"We can only have three, so one of y'all needs to go," one director said. He motioned at me and another guy—one hundred pounds smaller than me—to do a head-to-head of the night's dance routine. And we did it, fifteen times in a row.

If I wasn't already glistening and gasping for air, I definitely was after ten splits, twists, and high-intensity knee-kicks in a row. Both me and my competitor made sure that every move, motion, and sound from our drum major whistles was precise. Though he was in better shape than me, I was keeping up, and I *knew* that I was a better leader—given his perpetual lateness and childish antics with other band members.

After three months of conditioning, and one hour of dancing

until my knees nearly gave out, I was cut. When asked for a reason, both directors said, "You just weren't as enthusiastic as him." Though they'd both told me for months that drum majors need to be good dancers and, most of all, good leaders, being eliminated cause I didn't have the endurance of a 160-pound teenage boy was the biggest blow I'd had to my confidence in all my eighteen years of life. Upon learning this, I involuntarily boo-hooed and requested to leave the band hall from the back door.

"This is bullshit," I typed a million times via Kik. I didn't want to quit band—the one extracurricular I shared with all my friends. I texted my kings with all my rage while flipping through my phone to find music to cry to.

The album *Channel Orange* by Frank Ocean had dropped two months prior, but cause I was so busy trying to put on my poker face for niggas who didn't actually want me to win, I hadn't listened to it yet. I planned to save all the music I needed to catch up on for after I made drum major. Since that ship had sailed, I said "fuck it" and huddled my sore legs close to my chest. I made a nest of myself under my sad-ass tear-soaked sheets.

My taste at that time was mostly Odd Future, Kanye West, the Weeknd's *House of Balloons* tape, and Jodeci (don't ask). Cause I saw so much of myself in Odd Future—a group of Black kids who dared to do shit mostly attributed to white people—I kept up with their every move, ready to mosh at concerts and ride my skateboard around the tire plant close to my house while consuming their angsty content. Eighty percent of my listening that summer was the Odd Future tapes, *Purple Naked Ladies, Bastard,* MellowHype/High, and the "Oldie" video on repeat. I also listened to *Goblin* in secret since niggas thought Tyler was devil-worshipping or something. So it made sense to give Frank's new project a chance, since he was part of the tradition that had fit who I was at that time so well.

Channel Orange was different from the rest. My kings had told me it was "mid," but I wanted to listen for myself. From the "Start," I felt emotions I'd never allowed myself: reflection, nostalgia, and queerness. I'd learned that in order to survive my hood, Stop 6, as a person with boobs and a vagina, you had to be either straight and girly, a lipstick lesbian, or a hard-ass stud. There was no in-between, since the in-between that still wasn't accepted was queerness. There were no elders to teach me about Stop 6, an under-resourced Black neighborhood of a city that disowned or resented you for being anything close to queer, so I folded into its mold and stayed as incurious as possible. I leaned into what everyone was calling me anyway—slurs I won't name here—so men lost interest in me (unless it was the lazy "I can turn you straight" come-on hurled at me from grown Black men while I walked home from school). I just wanted to survive.

The extent of what I'd already known about Frank Ocean was "Thinkin Bout You," the hook he sang on "Analog 2" with Syd and Tyler, The Creator, and the eerily beautiful "White," a version of which was also included on *Channel Orange*. I didn't even peep his mixtape *Nostalgia, Ultra* beforehand, so I went into streaming the LP with no expectations. The opening atmosphere took me to the backseat of my nigga Julian's pickup truck the spring before—all the nights we spent smoking weed and lying to our parents about where and who we were. The production of "Start"—the people laughing, clicks of the iPhone, and gaming sounds—was something like entering somebody's weird-smelling house while their parents were outta town and watching dudes I secretly wanted to smash play video games till their high wore off. If you know, you know how beautifully that captures Black boihood.

And then I listened to "Thinkin Bout You" again. Though this record was hilariously memed in the earlier days of social media due to its dramatic portrayal of love (google "a potato flew around my room"), it felt so vulnerable. And *real.* It didn't hit me till I listened to *Channel Orange* that an R&B record could make you feel close to a beloved through poetic lyrics, spacey production, and layered guitar strings with a man spilling his soul in falsetto. Frank Ocean didn't mention gender at all in "Thinkin Bout You." For the first time I closed my eyes and saw a lover in rotating gender presentations, holding all of me close.

Frank embodied all my awkwardness (*No, I don't like you, I just thought you were cool enough to kick it*) and my insecurity (*You know you were my first time, a new feel*) in three minutes. For the first time, I knew without doubt Black masculinity was queer. And I don't mean that in the "emasculating Black men" way (I think anyone who says this is silly). I mean that there was no place for my Black, fat, femme, masc, queer, trans self to be myself in this world. I mean that my Black, fat, queer, trans self can't be myself many places in this world, though there are many folks—Ocean included—like me.

My kings made it clear that it was "gay" to do something that Frank was doing: being tender with a nameless, bodyless beloved. Even if the beloved was a woman (fellas, is it gay to love a woman?), it wasn't okay for me to be me. Though everyone around us invalidated the existence of Black queer womanhood, we invalidated each other with our limited, man-influenced masculinity.

Both then and now, there is no world where Black masculinity is treated like something expansive and *real.* There is no world that exists where Black masculinity is "normal." In a lineup of me, my kings, and every Black boy I grew up with, you'll find some kind of desire, and wounds—many of which can be attributed to performing masculinity. We are queer by design, and in *Channel Orange,* it felt like Frank got that. In all my anger, disappointment, and sadness about not getting drum major, I teleported to a place where Black masculinity was layered with complex tenderness.

"Pink Matter" reminded me of the times in Julian's pickup with many, many pink skies. The lack of 808s, his harmonized vocals moving from octave to octave—all of it felt like the softest thing, and it held me closer than any record had before.

There's something about this track—joined by André 3000's rapping, on the surface, about pussy—that crystalized our queerness. Here, he recalls the body of a Southern Black woman, and how he, a Southern Black man, can handle all her curves with ease. Black women and femmes have bodies that intimidate the non-Black gaze (as do Black men and masculine people), so to say that he can love, and feel no qualms about, a Black woman that would "intimidate" others feels, well, queer.

Until my first listen of "Forrest Gump," the second-to-last track on *Channel Orange,* I had never heard a man sing a love song to and toward another man. I didn't know that it was possible for men to embrace loving more than one gender at a time—and in the same album, no less. Imagine me, a Black boi with no examples of queerness that didn't need to be hypermasculine, hearing that song. Imagine me finding myself in between the heartache of being rejected and the imagery of Frank's queer admiration.

Around the time his album dropped, Frank published an open letter on Tumblr saying his first love had been another man. And cause we didn't have Lil Nas X or Kehlani the way we do in the mainstream now (and they even *still* catch heat), this beautifully crafted letter got ridiculously homophobic responses. The opening sentence was "Whoever you are . . . wherever you are . . . I'm starting to think we're a lot alike." Yet Black people came from every nook and cranny to say that they were *not* like him.

"I'm not bumping him no more, bro. I can't do that gay shit," one of my kings said as if we weren't also queer. It's as if this album didn't transcend harmful ideas of what people thought Black gay manhood was. Though Ocean's never said this, I remember the response being terrible. Many headlines said his coming-out was career suicide, and at my high school many Black boys refused to listen to him again. Queer-antagonism took over my peers'—and the world's—better judgment.

In *Channel Orange,* Ocean declined simplifications—of his sexuality, and of what R&B as a genre could say or do. Despite the negative messages around me, I was dialed in to his message.

When I first listened to this beautiful album, its songs started formulating questions I'm still finding answers to. The entire album was so healing, and it came to me at the best possible time. I was able to make more sense of myself, and how I wanted to continue to queer the idea of what Black masculinity could be. I started the years-long process of shedding the shame I felt for not being masc enough, or straight enough, and found language for my multiple-gendered desire.

Even if there was no one "like me" at my high school, there were folks like me in music. Ocean was one of them.

> *I wish you could see what I see* spoke to me, and, now, I finally think I do.

After that summer, I went on to stay in band as a section leader until I graduated. Then I went to undergrad and gained more language that contextualized my experiences. Ten summers later, I'm wearing what I wanna wear and sleeping with who treats me well. My life's work as a writer, workshop facilitator, and cultural worker is to make Black people, queer people, and masculine people fall in love with who they are and shed the daily violence of betraying themselves and others. Though I'm lucky to have found some of me in *Channel Orange,* there is still work to be done, so I organize, teach, and create art that aims to move toward a world where marginalized people find themselves sooner, and under better circumstances.

Kids like me were tasked with concealing so much; Ocean taught me to sit with those unspeakable feelings, and to speak them. Now I put *Channel Orange* on when I need a reminder of my inherently Black, inherently queer personhood. I'm transported to a remote soundscape with sultry vocals, airy instrumentals, and colorful harmonies—where expansive, untemplated masculinity for Black men and masculine people reside. Freedom for Black masculine folks sounds like polyphonic interludes, every gender getting the love that they need, and an album that needs no "coming out" statements. Just a full embrace for the moment of genius that it is.

Maybe that'll exist one day in outside-of-*Channel Orange* land. Until it does, I'll be visiting there, one spin at a time.

Girlhood

Walking forward backward sideways on top of
Adjacent to the land any land beneath the groundwater
Of land walking around they are
Watching me
While I stop at Malls, take pictures with friends
At the bar, picture me: walking into a tree
Watching them watching me
They are watching in a small jeep
slowing down next to me to ask
Do you need a ride to where you're going
I say that I am 17
Not enough to slow him down, not
Enough to uncapture me Is it what sits
Between my belly & my knees that keeps them
Watching me
No matter our race, but especially my race
Makes me lace under the starlit moon
A treasure ready to be seeped into
When an unfamiliar hand meets my shoulder,
Once again, I am 5
Or 10
Or 16
Feeling a presence, hearing it smile
Watching me

There Are Men Around

In 2013, I started to believe that there was nothing I could do to un-satiate a man's taste. I was a senior in high school, now carrying on me full, fat hips. For the nine years of growing that had happened since ten years old, I had been modest—almost to a fault—due to body shame, butchness, and constant chiding from my mother. The only man in my house was my father, so I didn't understand how her insistence that I consider that "there are men around" was actually applicable to my life, yet after a couple moans and groans, I would listen.

All the clothes that I wore were from the "men's" section of Hollister. I thought that I made it abundantly clear through the way that I dressed, talked, and walked that I was interested in women.* Neither my mother nor dad was approving, since they both were avid churchgoers and Black Texans dipped in the stench of queerphobia. Since I had my own money from my minimum-wage job at Braum's ice cream shop, I did and wore whatever the hell I wanted to. Despite my overexertion of masculinity, I still couldn't go to a corner store without getting crude remarks from boys and, mostly, grown men.

"Damn, baby! You gotta stop playing gay and getchu a *real* nigga," men who looked no younger than thirty would say from the passenger seats of hoopties. Scrubs, I tell you.

"Can I give you a ride home?" even-older brothers said while I sat on concrete curbs, smelling like dairy and hormones, waiting for my mama to pick me up after shifts at the shitty ice cream store.

* I now know that butchness does not equal "lesbian," but at the time, it was the only definition that I knew existed.

"Quit playing before I turn you straight," a football player at my school once said in an effort to get back at me for calling him a bitch. This was the earlier days of Twitter, when it was less regulated than it is now, so his post became a pile-on session about my body.

I was labeled *girl.* That was enough to always get unwanted attention from boys and men.

So why did my mama give me all this hell? Even more confusing, why did she do it at home? I still remember, vividly, the second time I asked her "Why, Mama?" when she told me "there are men around."

Finally, after a too-long back-and-forth, she answered, with a solemn, disgusted face I'd never seen her make before.

"Men are dangerous, baby. They do and say whatever they wanna do and say. You need to keep safe," she said. I still didn't understand, so I prodded.

"What do you mean 'men are dangerous'? We are around Dad, my uncles, your dad, and other men all the time. I just want to be able to walk around the house—this house, where only you, me, and Dad stay—with my cartoon draws and an undershirt on sometimes. It's hot!" I said, tryna make light of her clearly darkness-fused mood.

"Dad's not dangerous, but—ugh," she said in a frustrated tone. "You don't understand," she explained, then cut her eyes and retreated back to the kitchen where she was ironing Dad's work clothes.

I never thought of my dad as dangerous, per se. A two-faced asshole, yes; a dickhead, for sure, especially when he didn't have an audience to entertain. But dangerous? Shit, the only thing he's ever done that's felt dangerous is whooping me too hard one night I came home high and told him, "You get on my damn nerves" to his face. I wasn't ever scared of him. I guess she meant that most dudes are not my dad, and that many dudes consider violating you to be something as inevitable as you having a body.

I could agree, yet I knew it wasn't just that. I carried my body like a "damn dyke," according to many of my schoolmates and strangers, and still I was undressed by the eyes of boys and men on the regular. I don't know a girl who didn't have boys and men after them, treating them like a thing to be conquered—no matter how they dressed, or spoke, or closed their legs, or didn't. Gender-based violence is not an issue of optics.

After our talk, I took a shower and went to sleep.

Two thousand twenty-two. Twenty-two years after my first assault at five years old, nine years after the realest conversation I had with my mom, and a year and some change into being on hormone replacement therapy.* In 2022, most Americans are subjected to a lot more shit that exposes the sinister sentiments of American men. I can't scroll past a picture of a famous woman in *literally any attire* and not see a man sexualizing her. Even worse, these men tell women that they "shouldn't be so sexual," and that any abuse they experience is their fault because of how they dress. Though, in 2022, I was two years into a journey that pushed me to being perceived as one of those same men, I have a history of *womanness* in me. I know enough about that experience to know that it doesn't matter what you wear. "There are men around" is a statement too commonly rolled out of the mouths of women and femmes in order not to admit there is a man problem that's been alive and diseased for centuries on American soil.

* Moving forward, I will use the shorthand, "HRT."

Still, when I blink too quickly, I see the faces of the Black boys that assaulted me. I see the cars of those Black men that asked me to "get in" as a teen. I see the tongues of those Black uncles, cousins, grandfathers, sons that thought it cute of them to make sexual gestures at me while I was getting a Hi-C and some smokes. I should not be scared to wear anything cause there are men around. My mother—always respectable and safe—should not be weary/small/distant from me, her child, cause of what men need to huddle together and figure out. Men must question and resolve their need for domination. They must want—more badly than they want to make everyone not-man uncomfortable—to be well. Yeah, yeah, #NotAllMen (eye roll), but there are too many nonviolent men that don't check the violent men around them. That is also a type of violence.

If I could do it all again, instead I'd direct all questions to my dad. Me—a young, impressionable *girl* wondering what I need to shrink myself for—asking the man that chose to raise me all my questions about men. Here would be the remix:

"Close your legs, girl. There are men around."

In 2000, anytime adults said something I didn't understand, I answered with a "Why?"

"I don't know, ask your father," my mom said, still in a cheerful mood. I went home and asked my father the same question.

"Cause we're American, baby," he said, while looking at me in my love-filled eyes.

"Why, Dad?" I said back.

"Cause we were taken by white folks to this land, and have found ourselves trapped here since."

"Why, Dad?"

"Cause Blackness is synonymous with brokenness, and no matter how hard Mama and I have worked, we still in this old house we bought when we were twenty-three and twenty-four."

"Why, Dad?"

"Cause if we own something, we should keep it."

"Why, Dad?"

"Cause we been owned for so long, I and my granddad's granddad can't remember a time we weren't."

"Why, Dad?"

"Cause white folks took out stock in our memory. You know what we didn't forget, though? Misogyny."

"Why, Dad?"

"Misogyny the only thing that makes a Black man feel superior. All we wanted to do was live, and somewhere down the line, some Black men thought ourselves so small that we emulated white men."

"Why, Dad?"

"Cause they taught us we weren't enough. Me and you are enough, though."

"Why, Dad?"

"Cause we said we are, and imma keep teaching you that you're enough. I'm sorry for the state of Black men, but we'll get better."

"Why, Dad?"

"Cause we can't wait on them to get better. We got to. I love you."

"I love you too, Dad." The curtains would've fallen, and we both would've taken our bows.

Instead I'm here, fifty stars and thirteen stripes of trauma later, telling men to do better.

You Can Call Us, But

after Gwendolyn Brooks & Erykah Badu

we won't pick up the phone. We
're gone away for college. We
close up shop on our hearts. We
loose from the family chains of queerphobia. We
lose all people that love us badly. We
sing hotep songs walking to the Fort Worth club. We
visit each other's hands when dancing silly in the club. We
visit our family when they guilt-trip us enough. We
introduce our college friends, mix them into a friend stew. You
smoke till your eyelids can't keep up with you. I
fill the flask & free cups past the brim. We
sloppy-sing "Tyrone" till the air is unsaid truths. We
tell the truth, but we have to like you first. We
'll have babies if we're still lonely at thirty. We
end the night making ourselves pretty spectacles. We
going straight to hell if it's queer & got decibels. We
end the night drunk in love & susceptible. We
bend each other out of shape.

Our Allegiance to Queerphobia

I park my car in front of my off-campus apartment and run to the front door. I'm on my way to a show, or to pick up my girlfriend who works a walking distance away, or on my way to meet a friend who is losing it in this hellscaped school—regardless, I'm in a rush.

To my right is a Black couple, sitting in the patio area of a coffee shop next door. At this point in my fat, Black, masc, lesbian life, I've learned to ignore the feeling of eyes on me. You know, when you know you're being ~~eye-fucked~~ stared at so you do anything but meet those falsely curious, likely fearful, gawking eyes with your own. It's always somebody making it clear with their pupils that I'm wrong, that I'm a Bad Black (two perceptions that integration and gay marriage legalization didn't solve), so I ignore it; keep it pushin'; all the cool expressions you could insert for being uncurious and avoidant.

I don't know why I looked up. Maybe cause they were Black, though I grew up with only Black folks in my life till I started college. That changed nothing; Black folk still thought I was wrongness personified. Maybe cause a nice headnod to another Black person in an 80 percent white school environment is why we don't all drop out, or dissociate all day, or go more insane than generational trauma has already made us. Maybe cause I thought I had to get something from the car, so I did a weird looking-around thing as if the lost thing would reappear in the general vicinity. Regardless, I looked up.

Their eyes said fear. Then that fear—mixed quickly with the kind of superiority white supremacy loves to breed in anyone forced to believe in this shit way of experiencing other humans—dissolved into laughter. I saw my humanity melt away and become an object to them, first through fear, and then through their minds saying, *I'm better than this person.* (Is "better" just *more normal*? Is "more normal" just *more congruous with white supremacy*?) They were at least decent enough to not laugh in my face, so I quickly jiggled my keys and went inside.

Wild. It is wild how I knew, after twenty years of existing in this body/mind/truth, that my presence would always be perceived as wildness. Cause of this, I tried for fifteen out of my twenty years to force-feed femininity, traditional *womanhood,* to myself like a sick child. I was pouring it up for myself—through dresses, misogynistic boyfriends, blouses from Aeropostale, and fierce denouncements of *being gay*—and it went down like cement. Regardless, to outsiders, I was failing at "resisting my urges." Gender and sexuality are *urges,* right? Ones I had but never wanted. More than anything, I wanted to be safe, but safety isn't given to people as *wild* as me. I picked up my girlfriend's hat, or my friend's hat, or picked up my water bottle, and headed back to my car.

Before I knew its anthem or pledge, I knew what my nation expected of me. *Get in line. Put on this performance. Make sure you keep up.* This nation asks Black folks to tap-dance, keep up without ever stopping for ~~breath / life /~~ water, and scolds us with laws and loss for being tired. I knew that already. Every person with a Black phenotype that white members of this nation overtly and covertly hate knows that.

I couldn't have prepared for those same people—*my* people who know *my* pain cause it is *their* pain, *my* people who know how hot the pavement feels on bare feet in the fourth hour of improv body movement for white people—to hate me for failing to meet those expectations.

Anti-queerness runs through Black families like dance crazes; shimmy and shame, dilapidated disco moves, sad spins. In a 2021 Twitter video, Black women were asked, "Would you rather find out your man is cheating or bisexual?" and an overwhelming majority said the former. Sadness electric slides through blue circles of Black America. In a 2005 study, Elijah G. Ward posited that queerphobia runs deep in Black churches and Black nationalism rhetoric. Most Black people make hating queer Black people look like a conga line, a natural cutting of a rug.

The false prophets who have three women they lay with, the hoteps with nothing of substance under their multicolored hats, the ladies trying too hard to get picked—they all think I'm behind some "LGBT agenda." When they enact this violence on Black queer and trans folks, they are saying that they care more about their bigotry than they do about freedom. With their blistered feet they *tap-tap-tap* on me, and on every queer and trans person, when they make easily refutable claims. That's unfortunate, given our shared struggle, given that Black dance floors pinch, crackle, and rupture the same—no matter our gender or sexuality. Nobody's asking me the last LGBT meeting I went to before they do something anti-Black to me.

The walls of my apartment lobby were paper-thin. Surely some unbecoming cosmic force, one that didn't want me to have fun or feel safe that day, conspired with the couple's conversation. I involuntarily listened as they spewed more inquiry into my life.

"Do you think it's a girl or a boy?" the Black man said.

"Girl, I think," the Black woman said, with a chuckle that followed. There I was, naked in my wildness, genitals and sadness hanging for the world to see. I had an idea of what this couple, and the country, thought about me, but I didn't imagine it would be like this. Some conversation over sandwiches at a college. Hatefulness so natural that it can be spoken for any passerby to hear.

"Well, let's see when it comes back out."

It took me ten minutes to muster up the moxie to walk outside. There was no back door, and I couldn't give up my ~~life~~ car and every plan I had for my busy day to stay stuck in the lobby forever. I couldn't go back home. I had no home in the first place. And so I walked out and prepared myself for their bet.

Tap, tap, tap. My slow-moving feet sounded off from the gray pavement. Their heads turned like they'd just heard a bell saying "Dinner's ready." I turned my head too, but in the opposite direction as if I'd heard someone calling my name. I wanted their view of me to be obscured. I tripped over my own foot, luckily not hitting the ground but stumbling visibly enough for them to let out a chuckle.

This moment, and many moments I spent being butch and perceived by the world, was hell on earth.

"You was right!" the Black man said. He admitted that he'd lost the bet, a bet that shouldn't have happened, on whatever set of pronouns they thought I was that day.

Why aren't we all pissed?

Gender is a social construct, meaning we buy into it and it sells. The World Health Organization says that gender "varies from society to society and can change over time." Gender is not sex (male/female/intersex), and it is not based in any biological reality. Gender is quite literally something that early colonizers made up when they set norms for the United States, and even those norms—what we wear, dress, and how we speak—have changed, significantly, over time.

Gender is the most human thing ever. White men from forever ago told us "this is how things are," and we've let it lead to inequalities in class, healthcare, bodily autonomy, literacy, and the ways we treat each other—intercommunally and otherwise. I've never been a part of a Black community, at least one that has Black cishets—that didn't have queerphobia issues. Since before I can remember, I've been fascinated with—and scarred by—the sacred practice of queerphobia in Black culture.

From comments that denounce masculinity in Black girls to Black people enabling violence against any Black boy that dares to show an ounce of femininity, Black cisgender women and men have perfected the craft of shriveling up Black queer joy, un-aliving Black transness, and stifling the creation of Black children due to their prim and practiced, napkin-folded bigotry. We could blame the church, colonization, trauma passed down from generation to generation, but excuses won't keep Black queer people alive. Excuses won't get us free. While accepting a GLAAD Media Award, Kerry Washington called out queerphobia in Black communities specifically, by saying:

"So when Black people today tell me that they don't believe in gay marriage . . . the first thing that I say is, 'Please don't let anybody try to get you to vote against your own best interest by feeding you messages of hate. And then I say, 'You know people used to say that stuff about you and your love. And if we let the government start to legislate love in our lifetime, who do you think is next?' "

Who do you think? Who do you pledge allegiance to?

What makes queer- and trans-antagonism from Black folk especially hurtful is the cognitive dissonance. It's as if Black queer and trans people are somehow outside the *normal* that Black liberation will bring. It's as if there is such a thing as *safe* Black people. We're all unsafe in the eyes of anti-Black U.S.A. We are all unsafe no matter how cishet or respectable we appear. I knew this when I looked, through a corner of my disappointed eyes, past those homophobes and toward my car. If the fight of Black liberation is truly about equality, equity, and justice, then it needs to be that no matter what other characteristics a Black person has—gender, sexuality, ability, and otherwise. If we want non-Black folk to stop making assumptions about Black folk's humanity, then why aren't we ceasing this four-hundred-years-long party we've been forced to dance at, together?

Why aren't we all pissed?

When I walk from my car to my apartment, when I'm ready to ~~take a hammer to the foundation of the wooden floor / take a hammer to heads of people who want to keep me poor / take a seat and catch my breath after I've worked up a sweat I've opted into producing /~~ take a hat to a lover or a friend, can I count on meeting someone who understands what it's like to be doing everything we do to correct the queerphobic tongue when it flicks violence onto me? Can I do a simple arrangement of tasks without queerphobia coloring my day into Black—Blacker than my skin and the simple tasks that turn terrible with every added awful perception? Can everybody be rightfully pissed when one of us is violated; can some of us not continue to be violated by our own people?

I want to hold you, all Black people, in my arms. I want to grow old with you. We want to pledge allegiance to something new. It is past time that you—those who hold too close the need to be superior—let us.

I came to run away from Fort Worth but maybe also to have sex

What I mean is I was a repressed enby
who wanted to try a penis once
& needed to go somewhere that wouldn't reward
straightness; Austin could've been anywhere
but here I am, real enough to make everyone
uncomfortable. It is love

that's kept me wanting things that don't want me back
like Black men & answers for all my illnesses?
I have anxiety & want to be loved. I was too sick w/ boi,
thrashing like a child in the womb after the water breaks,
having trouble learning directions to places since
I dreamed my way through grade school.

I think I'm the fattest person with a big heart in this place;
that's gotta count for something—a name change
or a whimper. Diary of a Fat Black Kid with a Disability
That Went Unchecked for Too Long—that's my book.
I had to move away to give birth. I had to move to make space

for something ready to cry & mine all mine & page one
of my eventual love letter reads:
All I need is to be touched.

You Just Haven't Met the Right Guy

At one point, I believed them. By "them," I mean my mother, father, bullies at school, and religious leaders who tried to convince me that I'd started exhibiting characteristics unbecoming of a straight cis girl—liking dirt, hating skirts, etc.—cause I just "hadn't met the right guy." But I did meet guys; had sex with them, too. I started fooling with the alleged-opposite sex as early as eleven—starting with a boy named TJ.

It was sixth grade. I was still hanging out with the ~~stupidest bitch ever~~ predatory then–ninth grader named Lyriq from my first childhood church for cool points when a boy messaged me on MySpace. He thought I was cute and asked me a series of questions. I remember making a MySpace page like it was yesterday. This was back when everybody was a low-key coder, and little girls spent hours applying glitter GIFs, calligraphy, and a song that autoplayed so that anytime people went to our little free side of the internet, it emitted *girl.*

"Put the girliest pictures that you have up," Lyriq said. I had none, so three weeks prior to TJ messaging me, we staged a photo shoot in her smelly, poster-filled room.

~~Her~~ Our goal was to get a boy that looked like Lil Romeo to hit us up on MySpace. To achieve that, Lyriq posted Picnik-filtered pics in a push-up bra and clothes she stole from Family Dollar. She was a glutton for attention, and my introduction to everything terrible about being a girl. I was eleven, still figuring out what it meant to be what she called a *woman,* so I followed her ill-informed advice every chance I could.

TJ was from Virginia. The second he hit up my messages, Lyriq concocted this whole plan for how it would go.

"You need to be prissy, not-needy, confident, not-a-ho," she said, "since a ho is a girl who got all the boys in a *bad* way." She gave me a roadmap, with no input from me or anyone outside of what she consumed on BET.

"Hey baby, how u doin? U got a man?" TJ asked.

"Naw. Not yet XD," I shot back, Lyriq hovering over my keyboard, instructing me on what to send.

"Well why don't we fix that? Here's my number: ____________. Call me after school tomorrow." Lyriq and I jumped in glee. Finally, off the strength of my over-directed pictures, with poses of one corner of my face, on MySpace, a boy was giving me attention!

We talked on the phone most days while I waited for my mom to pick me up from my granny's house. Besides the occasional listen-in on another line from Granny (this was when all extensions of a house phone were connected), I kept our relationship very private. In a way, TJ was my solo experiment, my opportunity to figure out who I was in relationship with the gender that I was taught I should *only* be with, romantically and sexually. Who was I as a girlfriend, as a potential wife? In many ways, mothers (and aunties) (and other girls) (and systems) train girls to be good wives. Usually, I rebelled against said training at every turn. After school with TJ, though, I felt like I could be those things: a wife, a mother; I felt like I could make a good life with this dopey boy from Virginia. Even though I stumbled over my words, unsure of what to say to woo my new boo, TJ told me he loved me after two weeks—we were eleven, after all—and I thought that I'd won.

Despite all the nags for me to be "more girly," "more feminine," "less sporty," and the like, this boy said that he loved me. And he loved me for *me* (or at least, the little he knew about me based on my two MySpace pictures, Lyriq's overbearing coaching, and our surface-level conversations on my granny's house phone). Feeling confident after this assertion, I uploaded a new profile picture to MySpace while at my granny's house after coming home from school.

I didn't have time to run the pic by Lyriq, but I was sure that didn't matter much. This picture was more of a representation of everyday me: wearing black sweatpants, sporting my hair up in a ponytail, and wearing a somewhat-wrinkled white T-shirt. Unlike all my other pics on MySpace, this one revealed my entire eleven-year-old body. I was sitting in a chair in my granny's house, somewhat smirking at the camera. Minutes after I posted it, I got a message from my boyfriend TJ.

"Hey. I'm not sure if this is gonna work out anymore /: I'm real busy at school and we live too far away so it's probably best we end it."

"What?" I said, confused. "You literally just told me you loved me yesterday."

"Yeah /: I'm sorry baby."

At this point, I was fuming. I said something that I may regret for the rest of my life. "Fine then. You aint that cute anyway."

"Please I was letting you off easy cause you look like a dude," he said, then deleted me from his Top 8, then blocked me on MySpace (this is how I learned you can block people), and there it was: the uninhibited truth. A truth that I remember being one of the many knives I spent more than a decade digging out of my confidence. My first boyfriend broke up with me cause I "looked like a dude."

What do I do with this pain, I thought. I studied my new picture for hours. The lighting and angle, the contours of my face—was the alleged manliness in my cheeks? My slightly damp upper lip? Did he think my upper lip had hair on it? I started somewhat-seeing that in the picture. Was I sitting too manly? My aunts and mother had told me that before. So many people told me that who I was was wrong before. Maybe this boy just confirmed it. *There's something wrong with me and maybe it's that I'm too dude-like,* I thought for years.

I spiraled. I cried with my granny's bedroom door closed. After Granny left the living room long enough for me to dart to her newly cordless house phone, I dialed up Lyriq to get a second opinion.

"Hey," I said, dipped in melancholy.

"Hey girl, what's up," she said while eating what sounded like a million chips.

I paused for a moment, trying to figure out how to play down the embarrassment of the situation. "Have you seen my new picture on MySpace?"

"Yeah! Not something I would've picked but, you know, do you, girl," she said. Of course she said this shit. She'd usually have me obstructing three-quarters of my face to hold a peace sign over my mouth, or she'd have me showing only my eye and forehead from above.

"Okay. The boy I've been talking to broke up with me."

"Forreal? You sound sad. I didn't even know you were feelin' him like that," she spat out, then continued, "We not supposed to date boys super seriously from the internet."

This surprised me. Was this some girl-code shit that I wasn't privy to? "Well, how the hell was I supposed to know that?"

She sighed. "Damn, do I gotta spell everything out?"

I don't know what I was expecting from a phone call with Lyriq, but surely she knew how to make a bad feeling I was having worse.

After a couple more unhelpful quips, I hung up the phone with her and swaddled a pillow, crying on and off all night. Again I was confronted with the familiar feeling of inadequacy. I wallowed in this demeaning disappointment while I waited for my mother to come get me.

And then there was Jacob. Slender, tall, and yellow with a smile sunnier than the big thing that hangs in Texas skies. He was "the right guy" personified—at least on paper. He was an eighth grader who always said foul things to all the girls we shared last period band class with.

"Damn, Mama. When you gon' let me tap that!" he blurted to Ashley, the eighth-grade flutist.

"Baby, who let you out the house with them jugs jugging around!" he whispered with a mischievous laugh to Amber, the seventh-grade trombone player who was almost as quiet as me. He often reserved these comments for slivers of time when no adult was around to suspend him. Jacob often said the nastiest thing that came to his mind, and was backed by the snickers and handshakes of boys half his size that hovered around him like flies. Most girls saw him as a menace, and rightfully so; I saw Jacob as an opportunity to beat the "dyke" allegations, a boy shallow enough to give attention to any girl within his hormonal gaze.

"Hey girl," he said from behind me while I was unlocking my locker. He was, for some reason, on the seventh-grade wing. We were conveniently the only kids in the hallway.

"Hey," I said nervously. This was no flattery to him; I was nervous around anyone.

Another thing Jacob liked to do was dry-hump girls he found attractive. Somewhere between his vulgar comments and girls responding with disdain or silence or both, he would bend said girl over and straddle her jeans, or do the infamous *I eat pussy* hand motion with his mouth and fingers. He was exactly the right guy to try not being gay with, on paper.

I was unsure of what to do next. The look of hunger in his eyes told me I was in a vulnerable state. At this point, we were three weeks into the new semester and everyone who knew me was resigned to the idea that I was gay. Even though I'd never kissed anyone, or dated anyone; even though I was too scared to smile or laugh at anyone for an entire year. I worked overtime to wash off my face any of the girl-on-girl fantasies that played in my head, and the interest I had in the one butch lesbian's haircut and daily attire. I stared, blankly—at friends, teachers, classmates, and Jacob.

There were about two minutes before the lunch bell. I could make a run for it, or I could let him hump me and get caught by half of the school. Decisions, decisions. The latter would, I hoped, save me.

"Where are you going after this? Why is it not in my bed?" Jacob spat out. It took every bone in my face to hold back an eye roll.

"I don't know. To lunch, like most other people," I said, putting on my best impression of flirty banter. My palms were sweaty. I was carrying three heavy textbooks. In five seconds flat, the books were on the ground and he was humping the crack of my ass through my jeans.

Ring! Rrrrriiiiiinnng! The lunch bell sounded and classroom doors swung open. We quickly separated, but the (good) damage had already been done.

"Ooooh!" an anonymous face called out as he assessed the clearly nefarious optics. By the time I picked up my bags and headed to the cafeteria, I heard "Jacob" and "girlfriend" and "what just happened" more than a few times whispered by my peers. A whoosh of cold air washed over my face as I flung the cafeteria doors open.

Relieved didn't feel like the right word, but it was pretty close to my new feeling.

I was the fifth person in the "hot line"—a line where middle schoolers who weren't interested in the stale, often-soggy regular lunch could get hot wings, pizza, cookies, and other trash food for a reasonable price. My usual go-to order was five dollars flat. You had to be at least tenth in line to be guaranteed a fresh batch of hot-line food. You had to be twentieth to even get anything, cause it was junk, and we were all sweaty preteens; those foods didn't last long around us. A fresh, non-queer rumor about me was circulating while I was getting good food. *Lucky me,* I thought. Lucky me for letting a boy violate me.

Naturally, this rumor made Jacob pink in the face. He wanted the liberty to hit on *everyone,* not just the weird fat Black girl in his band class. No matter how many times he dispelled it, or how many other girls he hit on as a counterpoint, everyone wanted to believe he had a girlfriend, and that it was me, so they did. It was unbelievable and salacious enough to stick around for the better half of four weeks. Anytime anyone saw us close to each other in the hallway, someone twisted it into a make-out session.

One day we were the last few people left in the band room after the end-of-school bell rang, and all of a sudden people thought we'd done it in a clarinet room. It was wild, seeing other people get so worked up about my nonexistent love life. "How'd you do its" came to me from the popular girls. Mean jokes came to him from his jocky, too-cool friends. We were in a fake relationship, getting two wildly different experiences. That was until he'd had enough, and really laid some harsh words of truth on me in the hallway.

"I'm tired of this rumor, and I'm tired of looking at your Black face!" he yelled at me. Calling someone "Black" in those times—

despite us going to a 98 percent Black school—was the biggest insult one could get. Well, the biggest insult behind calling someone gay.

"We were never together. I just wanted to make the weird lesbian my jump-off," he daggered and twisted. This was during a passing period, and at this point, since everyone was nosy as hell, everyone—including teachers—was staring. There were many times in my childhood when someone disrespected me and I was too shocked to say anything. This was surely one of those times.

"I never wanna see you again!" he sneered.

"You weren't sayin' that when you were humping her in the hallway," Booger yelled. He was the meanest kid in my grade. His popularity surpassed Jacob's simply cause he had a neck tattoo.

"Her? For all we know, this could be a he," Jacob said, then walked off leaving me and everyone else stunned. Out of all the insults he hurled, everyone knew this was the worst one. This was the one that also hurt me the most.

I wore jeans, our uniform shirts, and even the occasional ribbon in my hair. Why would he call me a "he"? I looked as confused as everybody else. I was the only person who knew that it wasn't the first time I'd been accused of something non-*girl*.

I wanted to know how I could fix what was wrong with me. Some trumpet player that always made foul jokes now put me in an even worse position popularity-wise than I was in before. It sucked to be boxed into a sexuality I didn't even understand, to be so misunderstood that my essence made boys deny me a gender I so desperately wanted to embrace. I didn't know how to be a girl. I didn't know how to be a cishet girl, even when I showed interest in boys near and far. Jacob and TJ weren't the only guys that didn't end up being the "right guy," but they were my first flops. They were the tone set for ten more years of trying and failing to be the she/her expected of me.

Dating apps are kind of the worst. Especially when you're tryna find something serious. Especially when you're trying to find a quick fuck that isn't a weirdo serial killer or some despo cishet guy with too much of a past of being an incel to be any good in bed. But I used 'em anyway.

At twenty-two, I was new to Austin, Texas, and straight out of a years-long relationship with Gina. We were on-again/off-again and I tried to be on-again again, but she rightfully declined to put up with any more of my foolery. With iPhone data to use and a broken heart, I perused on Tinder, Her, and Bumble looking for America's Next Top Fodder to land my flailing body on. For the first time since my first boyfriend, I wasn't overly obsessed with romance.

Post-breakup, my needs were much more carnal. "Take off my Fruit of the Looms and rail me," if you will. It really was so simple. Up until this point, all my lovers had been femme-presenting cis women. I was ready to widen my sex pool to include men (again), just to see what could happen. I mean really, after your life trajectory has been destabilized, after the person you thought you'd spend the rest of your life lesbian-loving incorrectly says "no thanks," what else is better to do than start questioning your sexuality?

Being strictly v-on-v for seven years didn't stop me from having non-femme crushes. Butch girls, the occasional shirtless football player walking around campus, Idris Elba—I've always been a person with eyes, you know. When I re-downloaded the apps, I changed my settings to "all genders" just to see what might be out there. I wanted to see what bones I could jump, and what gender would reach out quickly to touch me. I just needed to be fucked. I just wanted some lust, to anti-love for a moment.

And then came Darius. Whew, Jamaican Darius had everything good: brown skin, long locs, a slender-yet-muscular body, a six-two frame, and a huge penis. I mean, if you put that thing in a picture next to his thigh in the right lighting, you might not be able to tell one from the other. When I first encountered him, it was through hazy pictures on Tinder. From the blur of his photos and the blunts that joined his plump lips in them I could tell he'd be, if nothing else, a good time.

I must confess something now. I was twenty-two, and had never had p-in-v sex. In my defense, I was a stereotypical butch lesbian during the time that everyone lost their virginity, so I lost mine, inevitably, to a cis girl. There was no space in my mind to conceive of ever having sex with a cis boy; not until now. Not until I was knocking on the door of Darius's apartment, all de-butched and scared enough to shit myself. He answered the door completely naked, with a blunt in his mouth.

In our messages I *did* say that I wanted nothing more than to bone, so it made sense, in retrospect, that he did this. I looked him up and down and walked through the barren apartment, shaking. Darius had no furniture in the living room, and his bedroom was nothing more than a futon, incense, and sheets turned into makeshift curtains covering some grimy windows. What had I gotten myself into? Bed with a nigga that for sure played some kind of sport in an earlier life. Bed with a nigga who would've called me a dyke if he saw me on the street last week.

He must've sensed my nervousness. As I stared at the bed in his room, he kissed me from behind. He rubbed circles into my shoulders and told me I looked "beautiful" today. I wore Goodwill booty shorts, a T-shirt, the only push-up bra/panties combo I owned, and a bandanna over my new locs. Niggas say anything. He asked me, softly, if I wanted my shirt removed. I said "Yes," damn near whispering.

He picked up a jar of warmed-up coconut oil and massaged my

back. I closed my eyes while he was doing this, in pure bliss. I was tense from breakup-then-moving stress, after all. He kissed my neck while breathily whispering:

"Do you wanna move to the bed?" His smells—essential oils, toothpaste, and horniness—made me warm and tingly. I felt his junk go stiff. I nodded and lay on his frameless mattress. We kissed until my shorts were off and he lay, naked, on top of me.

I'd never felt so naked—emotionally—until then. I mean, I was scared shitless. My legs seldom lay open like this (shout-out to my stone butches!), and they'd never lain open for a person with insertable, non-fingerlike genitals. Would I bleed? Would he think, all of a sudden, that my big, Black body was repulsive? I didn't know. I wasn't sure where to go from here, so I got all apologetic, like a girl would.

"Hey just a heads-up, I have this skin condition that makes the skin in my inner thighs darker—just so you're not freaked out by it. I shower and stuff every day," I said, basically under my breath. A nervous laughter escaped from my lips, and I immediately felt embarrassed. He looked back at me, patience coloring his brown eyes, and said:

"I don't care about that. I love your body, actually." He looked me up and down like a snack, or maybe a pillow he wanted so badly to lie in. I was unsure how to take the "actually" in that last sentence, but I chose to take it as a compliment.

"Thank you," I said, still nervous. My guard was coming down a tad. Darius explained that we only would do what I was comfortable with, and I convinced myself I was comfortable with everything. Everything? *Everything.* If I waited this long to do this, I wanted to not hold back. Anything expected of this experience, I wanted to do; *this* was the time I'd finally figure out if I just "hadn't met the right guy."

He put his bare dick in coconut oil (a bad idea, I now know) and then slowly coached it inside my airtight vagina, waiting for my cues to continue. He put it about halfway in and I was unsure I could go on. "Is there more?" I said, struggling to contain the fact that it hurt.

He chuckled, said "That's about five out of nine inches," and my whole life flashed before my eyes. I've never been a glutton for pain. Shit, I flinched when I got flu shots—whenever I worked up the nerve to get them. Is *this* what sex was—the stuff I sneaked to watch on my mama's OG Mac desktop? The stuff I watched in the dark with Lyriq when her parents weren't home?

Sucks if true, I thought. Still, I told myself I must continue.

To spare you further details, we went on with the encounter. My vag hurt for days afterward; I even peed blood post-coitus. I went home with a sense of accomplishment, though; I'd had sex with a cishet guy, and I thought the guy was cute even when his schlong was hurting me. Who woulda thought! After a couple more encounters, the pleasure came; before I even noticed it, I became a regular at bad boy Darius's apartment. When I wasn't working or sleeping, I was getting my back blown out by Darius.

Morning, midday—it didn't matter. Whenever our schedules synced, we were gettin' busy with it, and I mean *busy.* Most days, it felt like I was "getting away" with something—being a secret heterosexual, or maybe doing something I said so many times that I would never do. Besides the twenty or so people on my finsta and my roommates, nobody knew about this arrangement. I was proud, but also a bit embarrassed that I had caved in to this age-old homophobic idea of meeting the right guy.

Were they right—my mother, the church ladies, every bigot? Did I really just need to find the "right guy"? Unclear; about a month into our entanglement, I found a baby stroller in Darius's closet. When asked about it, he said, simply:

"She comes over here whenever her mama isn't trippin'." The "she" in question was his two-year-old daughter. The deadbeat dad of it all almost completely turned me off from him. What really put the nail in the coffin were the asks—"let's smash" and "you up?" turned into "can you take me to work"—and weird resentment toward me cause I didn't want to "hang" with him. I was a hookup, not a mother or Uber ride or girlfriend. He was the kind of man used to women falling all over him; the fact that I didn't was too much to handle. So Darius wasn't "the right guy," and neither were the other non-women who were lucky enough to get some from me while I was thotting and bopping around. I beat the ex-homo allegations.

If there was anything learned from my post-breakup expansion, it was that I wasn't a lesbian. I also learned that gender roles aren't perfect matches with "top" and "bottom," and that my body wasn't something to be hidden during all sexual encounters. My body was something I needed to (slightly) change in order to feel more comfortable. And once I made that change—getting top surgery*—if someone wasn't down to be with my naked and free body, then they weren't worth having sex with. The myth of "you haven't met the right guy" was incorrect the moment I said it was, and even when I did the exploring that homophobes said I needed to do—dating and fucking cishet men—the phrase still did not ring true. I'm grateful for (almost) all the romantic and sexual sitches I found myself in, cause they led to the stable sense of gender and sexuality I have today. But—and I can't say this enough—this exploration isn't necessary for everyone.

* University of Iowa Hospitals and Clinics defines top surgery as "the surgical removal of breast tissue and tailoring of the remaining chest skin, when needed, to generate a masculine chest contour. Usually, the surgery involves reducing the size of the areola, the darker skin surrounding the nipple."

We must believe people when they tell us who they are. We must create a culture where people's reality always overpowers other people's bigotry. There is no one on the planet who knows more about a person's gender or sexuality than that person does, and the fact that political and everyday bullies team up on queer and trans people to tell them that their reality is invalid sickens me. I don't know why so many folks are in a rush to be on the wrong side of history, but "haven't met the right guy" statements must cease.

I've been around the block. I've seen the emptiness leaking in these streets. Too many of us are compelled to accept genders and sexualities assigned to us; sex and romance would be so much more worth having if they were had on one's own terms. Less dishonesty means more love. Less coercion into certain sexual or romantic behaviors means that more examples of healthy, sustained relationships would exist for youth (and adults still parenting the kid inside of them). Maybe I'll never meet the "right" guy in this lifetime; maybe the right guy is me. Maybe he is the masculine fella staring back at me in the mirror, thinking of all my ex-flings with a smile, loving my partners in ways I know I can and will, giving them everything I was denied until I saved myself.

three

Toxic Masculinity

after Robert Frost & NeNe Leakes

`Name: Black boy`

There ain't a heart he hasn't broken
in this city. Though shitty men roam
from hospitals to rooms they make
vacant with their failures, he stood tall
& we thought maybe all our men-filled
disappointment would be solved
by a brother who makes the world shine
with his smile. Crooked & tall, he stays
casket-pretty. We stretched our hands out so far
to catch him. Every time he falls out of grace,
every time a new man emerges
just to be infected with this
Stone Age sickness, we call our daughters.
Ask how they are doing. Ask them
if they've seen the inevitable news.

`Place of death: America`

I know they loved me after all. Still,
I'm tasked with managing all this back-
handed masculinity. My inheritance:
attacks on everything, mandated;
my father passed down the right to be reckless,
to expect those "beneath us" to tidy
up our wreckage,

to tell ourselves the translucent remnants
of white supremacy on our skin
are a gender or sexuality's fault, that we must be
harder than walls to withstand its evermore pain.
I'm only obliged to me.
I'm not ashamed of anything.

`Cause: strangled himself to death`

Just shut the door behind they asses. Kick
the insidious scouts for next generation's
problems—peons passed down from one
broken man to the inevitable next. Just
cut the cord from Mary's belly.
Great monolithic knees, the misguided beings
kick back & watch their mothers stretch
their necks out again & again
& again, the family torn from the inside—

`with help of extension cord acquired`

In any event, the boy was found.
In a town where night grips
your toes while they dip from under covers,
begging for any cold air. He lived
in peace. He ripped
to pieces the day he learned
his father was the man
he thought he was. He cheated
on his mother, lied to maintain
lifetime dominance over people and things

that didn't ask for it & despised
the world for making him out to be closer
than thin sheets on a naked body in a morgue
to failure at all times.
Black is not the word for it. Neither is
inevitable, but that one's closer.

from grandpa's grandpa

The door is closed to men who wait to call
police, or call the streets to come collect
their kin, who think me something subhu-
man—book it; double-crooked; Black boys,
our Black boys, thirsty
like mad soldiers holding on to
something relevant to patriarchy's commands;
so comfy in their empty. Drinking on
my downfall like it was the Red Sea—god called
Said *teach these niggas how*
to do my deeds better. god is
a man after all like the father of a boy
I raised who never calls
'less it's for intent to harm
hard-earned harmony some other god sent
to heal us all from this one.

A 4th generation suicide tool

I can't wait to tell Columbus—
my father, the father of all hatred
in these states we call home—

he's lost. Though I can't taste the BBQ
of victory without his sauce. What is
victory if everyone's lost?
I'm lost without a need; I want
to decree C's dynasty dismantled,
but does that mean I'm free? That I
share? I want to help myself.

`disguised as gift`

Suppose there is a power struggle:
white man vs the world; colonizer vs
the things they decided to colonize. Too many
of them want to be god themselves.
Too many are too busy mandating laws
to break laws Nature—the actual god
they claim to call—put in place herself. *Help,*
said the Black boy drowning
in all his want. *Help me,* said the billionaire
who legally mandates all of our drowning.

`Name: Black man`

If ever there was a time to hate, too late;
They hate us always like they hate
the crate of cavalier monostophes
charging at their larynx. Especially the one
compelling a grown man—
no, a full-grown synonym for living
in hell, these states, this spell
enacted by white supremacy—

to cry. Who must die to hold
their cold door open? Who folds
the fidgety card table chair
bought for lie-99 into a thought?
Suppose that the Black boy is lost
without the fiery promise of
toxic power. In his quest, he asks—

Name: Black boi

Am I a god-fearing man? Am I happy?
Am I able to breathe? Am I single?
Will I let my masculinity, my masc-
beaten hands wrap around her waist,
take her down & drape her in all my
inheritance, greenery ~~her beautiful~~
my beautiful neck
with all of my fool's gold
till she goes sinking in quicksand,
the bed my grandpa's grandpa
named Columbus made
for me? Am I an earth-fearing man?

Name: Black boy
Place of death: America
Cause: strangled himself to death
with help of extension cord acquired
from grandpa's grandpa
A 4th generation suicide tool
disguised as gift

Name: Black man
Place of death: a state once stolen from Mexico
Cause: unnatural causes
Cause that started at "it's a boy"
Survived by: Christopher Columbus

Name: Black boi
Place of death: their mind
Cause: a chip on their shoulder
A belly that stayed empty
An empty bed cause of subscription
to Christopher's sins
Unwillingness to change
Pantomimed "traditional" manhood
A thing that's taught so can be untaught
Ballistic failure survived by:
a mother's hysterics
Multiple bruised & bloodied hearts
Bodies that wish they never touched them
A little girl-turned-boy's initiation
into a cult

Mountains are knees. Uphill,
a tree asks me if it will ever see
daylight not injured by a human's inner
misdeeds. Its mother burned in a fiery furnace;
my sister interred in a chamber making
decisions based on futures in her womb. My womb
making a run for it—

running the run-on sentence into oblivion
missionary mayhem Mickey Mouse mystery
mini me miming her death in front of a senator—
I think mountains are metaphors for the body.

There is no landscape we can call heaven.

Pretty*

These days I have hairy thighs. A hairy face. A hairy ass, back, and hair that makes it sting to take off a Band-Aid. I have a voice that vibrates when I speak, and a stocky stature that grows boxier every time I eat another chicken box. Most days, I get my clothing from the section that has the silkiest button-downs that don't highlight my shape too much. I am a formless body in my head, a form-full body of question marks to the rest of the local thrift store as I ask the closest register for the key. It feels earned, being masculine and ambiguous, having things hug my figure only when they're on the clearance rack. I owe it to myself to be pretty.

I go to the men's restroom, cut my eyes away from people standing up to pee, let the waft of death (read: *male piss*) violate my sense of smell, and carry on with my day like any sensible man would. When folk offer me the stand-up urinal, I say "I'm good yo, I have to shit" and clear out the restroom (80 percent of the time) like any sensible woman needing space. Once the bros and non-bros leave, I sit down and let today's perceptions wither away as I wipe my vagina and contemplate ripping off the Band-Aid again. I pull my pants up and continue this charade, this never-ending performance of gender. Second puberty looks good on me. So good that I pass as he/they or erased.

In 2015, I had the littest party that a ten-max-occupancy apartment in the whitest part of Fort Worth could have. It was junior year,

* This essay has been read, and signed off on, by the survivor of the abuse mentioned here. Take care of yourself.

and I swore that I was gonna be more social and not let my fear of being "the gay one" at every Black party—and "the Black one" at every other party at the private Christian uni I was attending in North Texas—stop me from building connections, even if they were fickle and only existent during hours that I should be studying. Co-hosted with my very straight roommates, I had bottles and a semi-sausage fest a week after moving into our small, thin-walled crib that cost $1,200 a month. After the nth shot of below-the-well vodka, I looked past my guillotine of acquaintances and saw a beautiful chick, stumbling and grinning at my front door with her sister. Her jet-black, stallion-like weave complemented her high-yella face. She had on the longest lashes I'd ever seen in my life. If chins could drop to the floor in real life, I would've been collecting mine off the sticky tile the moment we made eye contact.

"KB? It's Gina," she said. She was so pretty.

Truth be told, I don't think I've ever been a stud. My limbs are flimsy; I feel awkward in most situations where I have to speak to strangers, and girls like me in the way that they like black coffee: if they do, it's an acquired taste. When I came out, the girls flocked in droves and immediately changed their destination. If my skinny jeans didn't tell on me, surely my un-smooth pickup lines and insistence on quoting *Spongebob* every five seconds gossiped up the whole damn school district. I don't think I've ever been cool or close enough to the studs I knew and looked up to. One in particular I'll never forget.

I first met Kay at volleyball practice. My parents, insistent on the fact that me being tall and fat equated to me being destined to play sports, made me join my middle school's volleyball team. I hated the getup, the jiggle of my boobs when I had to practice spiking, and the long-as-hell serving lines forty girls (including me) had to sit in at 6 a.m. As we seventh graders strolled into our first day of practice, I remember Kay, serving up the strongest backhands to the ridiculously dented volleyball and quietly practicing her passing skills with the volleyball coach. Her freckled copper face lit up every time she threw the ball up for a smack.

I come from a family of sand-volleyball-at-the-family-reunion players. Truly, none of them—no matter how talented—quite served like Kay. I gawked, but not in the way that the others did. Kay's saggy basketball shorts and white T with a see-through sports bra caused quite the upset for girls in my grade.

Homophobic phrases snickered through the smelly serve line and all the way back to the coach, who said Kay's name out loud, as if to tell us she wasn't a *boy*. Her bald fade, mid-toned and still-prepubescent voice, the confidence in her presence, her self-celebration of difference so early in our middle-school experience, confused many of my peers who didn't know any better. Luckily, she didn't care what anyone thought. All the girls on Kay's team seemed to know this already. Based on her response to the coach, "I already know" with an eye roll, she expected us to be just as quietly violent as her team was on Kay's first day.

She wasn't interested in addressing it—the culture of queerphobia stinking up the place as much as preteens with no idea that Victoria's Secret doesn't mask stench. Her only aim was to show our rusty asses how to get at least one win that would help our parents make sense of spending eighty dollars on these hideous fits. Snickers and judgment aside, I think she might have changed my life. The fact that she was shopping in the "opposite" section of the clothing store, the fact that someone the world saw as *girl* could cloak themselves in whatever they wanted, that we have permission to reject all expectations of makeup and boy-talk and shave off all our fucking hair and look GOOD while playing an over-feminized sport, was something that hadn't occurred to me till then.

Discovering these wonderful facts was much more intriguing to me than listening to the worlds-old cheap shots cissies were taking at this beautiful Black girl. I didn't have the gusto to rock a fade until nine years later, but damn, maybe Kay taught me.

We had the wildest sex that night. To get Gina in my room, I think I said some wack shit like "You wanna see this painting?" and it worked (somehow). At this point in college, upperclassmen were promoting "ring by spring" propaganda: get the girl, lock her down with an engagement ring, then graduate together. Gina was an apathetic freshman, and I was contemplating dropping out all summer. If heaven was a glorified dorm room full of niggas I didn't know that well, then we were a match made in that bitch the night that we met. My psyche was scheming on how I could lock her down, treat our love like a shoo-in, imprint on her that I was *the one* while she slept, still in those lashes, without a bonnet to protect that beautifully pressed black hair.

She was so damn pretty.

People in my life have always given me mixed messages about what it means to be masculine. To my dad, it was breadwinning and honesty (depending on the setting). To my granddad, it was cheating on your wife for ten-plus years yet expecting everyone to beam with joy when they see you at family gatherings. To the studs who didn't like me for unclear reasons, it was regurgitating every boy's worst qualities—smelling weird, moving weirder—and aligning with womanhood as much as it wanted to with them. To my imagined biological father, it is not knowing that your daughter exists. In a way, I'll always be that daughter, in grown men's business, forcing myself to fit into my dad's smelly loafers at night, fitting into this world in my dreams and nowhere else.

Pretty is painfully relative. As an adjective, Dictionary.com says that "pretty" means "pleasing or attractive to the eye, as by delicacy or gracefulness." As a noun, "an attractive thing, typically a pleasing but unnecessary accessory." Though not gendered, we often associate prettiness with womanhood, femininity, and objects we see as *dainty*. I've never been interested in womanhood, but I've always wanted to be treated softly, like a fat pleasantry to the eyes. On both sides of the pummeled-to-death binary, I haven't been seen as *pretty*, at least not in the ways I wanted. When I was femme, my prettiness was canceled out by Blackness. When I was butch, my prettiness was seen as invalidating my masculinity. Who taught us that masculinity can't be pretty? Who taught us that Blackness was devoid of prettiness and delicacy?

Gina and I were young adults running on hormones and infatuation. I took her everywhere I went—Fort Worth, my trauma, and my chapped, hungry hands. And she did the same for all three years of our messy, unfortunate story. I can't remember a time I wasn't drunk, smoking weed, or spitting on sidewalks after forcing myself to take one huff of her vape, or as I called it, "scented cigarette machine." We mirrored each other when it did and didn't make sense to.

I needed a therapist but I had a girlfriend, damn pretty and ready to want me, instead.

I think of myself as a medium-good person, meaning I am good depending on who you ask. If you ask my current partner, I am good in all the ways she wants—draping her in my arms at night, saying "thank you" and "I'm sorry," telling her she looks beautiful in the moments her eyes say she wants it. If you asked Gina, I am the worst person alive and will likely die that way—she has years of unforgivable nights and days to prove it. If you ask me, I have let toxic masculinity drain me of my personhood so much that I, at points, was unrecognizable, committed to performing something someone else told me I should to the detriment of my people. If it was a thin line between Noah's list of people who made it onto his ark and those who didn't, I would've missed it by a couple of points. Funeral processions make sense. I'd like to think the lady clapping in the front seat as my carcass is carried out will be Gina.

I was the one that had the idea of her moving into my minuscule crib after her parents told her that being with me wasn't acceptable. I let her know of it during a double date to Six Flags, a place I'd never go if I was more honest back then. I slipped a Tums into my mouth (motion sickness) and took a swig of water in the front seat. I turned to her with something in my spirit that I thought I'd never felt: unconditional care for another human being. I demanded she tell me that she loved me.

"I know you love me; just say it," I said, with all the confidence of a cishet man. I somehow made up in my mind that because I had a bad bitch, I needed to butch it up.

"What do you mean?" she said, wanting me to just admit my feelings.

"I mean that I want to hear you say it," I said, arrogantly. This is how many of our fights started.

I spend most days trying to be the mentor I didn't have. The ~~father mother~~ person that would've told me that I needed to do better. The person that would've unraised my voice, packed and shipped away the unnecessary lies, showed me how to shave my itchy, patchy beard for the first time with the femmes around me breathing without headaches and indignities. The person, barely spiking a ball before embarrassingly walking to the end of the middle-school volleyball line, needed them. The perceived-as-man person I was for the first two years of my medical transition* needed them. The person who dated Gina needed them, especially as I confess who I was to you.

I could feel something different, something cosmic inside of me that I knew to suppress. Funny, when I was dating boys during my first and second year of high school, I didn't have the same confirmation. I didn't have the added pressure of being a boyfriend, a pillar of salted indifference, anything that wasn't a girl. Instead of telling Gina how much she meant to me, I wanted her to slip into forced vulnerability so I could feel bigger—why don't masculine people feel big when they are naked in truth? I've tried to be free in the years since our breakup, but this moment cost me too much. It haunted me like the socialization of something no man should become.

She said, "This isn't necessary," with fear overpowering the light brown in her eyes by three tons. If what I saw had a color and shape, "triangular with red tints all over" comes close. How I saw shittiness reflected and I wasn't fearful of it, how it made her breath become shallow and my temperature spike to an unhealthy degree, I don't know. My budding masculinity, my cloak of something over me, was the embodiment of abuse.

Do not care if I don't want to go dancing: I'll put my
left feet in cowboy boots, finish inching out of my shaggy
self-loathing, put on my shirt and ripped-up jeans

* There are multiple ways to transition, but usually when people say "my transition," they're thinking of "medical" or "social." When I say "medical," I mean using medical interventions (surgeries, hormones) to align my body/gender presentation with my gender identity. When I say "social," I mean telling people I'm trans, going by a different name than my birth name, and making other (legal/fashion/social) changes to live with my gender identity.

to feel you in my arms when Robyn sings about something you can't
relate to. Would love to tell you all of my secrets but if
I let them sit in the air then I have to be accountable to them. I can't be
that kid, that young adult, that monster in your eyes so I
keep my heart closed, do that under-the-bridge goth dance
that tears you into pieces every time. I'm not wealthy in conscience.
I cannot look myself in the eye or expect Gina to talk to me,
but I can tell you you're beautiful when I am so hot that I'm sweating
through the holes in my shirt. I am a commuter. I am grooving next to you
in a celestial world where I didn't do it and I sync with you guilt-free.
Too bad I am a sliver of myself and you'll never know.
You never know who you are till you do.

As the perception of me changes before my eyes, I realize that it is a specific sadness—embodying patriarchal masculinity in a country that wants your blood more than it wants you to breathe. Before I open my mouth, I am a conviction, a violence inflicted upon everyone around me. When I was a Black butch it was silent; now, it is louder than ever. Maybe that's why I evolved in that way, made it everyone's problem to love me, be loved by me, be done wrong by me. Especially Gina.

We moved in together when I was twenty and she was eighteen—young enough to not see past lust, and old enough to know what is and isn't acceptable. I would rage and gaslight till she became a quiet convenience. Anytime I struggled with an urge to cheat, I would become suspicious of her—from new friends to her exes and their intentions when hitting her up via text.

"Why are they contacting you," I'd say, as if she had a cosmic pull to stop someone from reaching out.

"I don't know. But I'm not interested in them. Only you." How could I believe her if I didn't want her fully? Some call it a Madonna-whore complex; I call it the socialization of toxic masculinity: seeing women as sexual desires or pure, virgin-like romantic suitors. At that point in my life, in 2016, I'd never met a Black man or Black butch woman that preferred a woman who was comfortable disagreeing with them. Or that's had sex with more than one other person. Or that expects emotional vulnerability from them—and we should talk about that more as a people. I had a boy emotionally and sexually violate me before I had a boy be honest about his desire for me. I saw butch women and straight or gay men fistfight, be arrested, gaslight their way out of accountability, before I saw any of them cry.

What does this world do to us? What do we do to ourselves?

My best friend of seven years died by suicide three months after Gina and I moved in together. His last text to me was something like "I've never seen you care this much about a girl." Then *boom:* all the softness I had detonated; it hardened up and crumbled. As I was packing up his belongings, taking what I wanted and driving the rest to his parents, I packed up all the want I had in my heart to be better, to be less of a mash-up of every version of masculinity that I encountered. There is no road map for a pretransition trans person in grief. There is nowhere I could put down my sorrow, nowhere I had ever seen it be placed except on the wives and mothers and partners of my brothers. I was fearful of my shittiness, yet embraced it.

My window of tolerance for disagreements slimmed from half of an opening to a crack. I said and did things to cut down myself and her; "abuser" is too mild a word for it. For not letting the cries that need to come out, come out. For making your emotional issues somebody else's trauma. Instead of medication and therapy, again, I had the prettiest girlfriend. A mother-type girl. A beautiful Black girl. Even if it—my ridiculous rage, my incessant need to control—only came when I was mad, or sad, or triggered, it came and I felt like I couldn't control it. My want to yell, my pathway from any emotion straight to unwarranted anger.

I was mad at the world for continuing without my friend breathing. I was madder at Gina for trying to talk to me about it, as if I ever learned the skill of processing. Every bad thing that happened to me as a child was mine—I didn't talk to my parents; I didn't have a therapist—therapy wasn't some shit my Christian boomer Black parents believed in. I remember the bruises I went to middle school with from my father that I was told meant "I love you." I remember the rumors of not being "butch enough," of "faking being gay" that studs started in high school cause I'd rather sport Hollister chinos and I told girls exactly how I felt. I remembered burying this, along with my abusers, along with my friend—a man I loved and never knew if he loved me back, since we didn't say those things to each other. *Volatile* is too small of a word. *Broken and afraid,* mashed up and force-fed to the part of me who didn't feel empowered to speak, comes close.

Once, in Intro to Spanish class, some girl was attempting to bully Kay. In the middle of conjugations, somehow asking them "why do you dress like that" made sense to this ugly-ass, childish-ass girl.

"What do you mean," Kay said, in the kind of sincere voice that also sounded concerned.

"Well, cause you're a girl. Girls don't dress like that," the girl said, gesturing at Kay's Levi jeans, Jordan 12s, and tall white tee.

"Cause I like girls," Kay said. It's as if the girl's entire life changed with four words.

"What?"

"I. Like. Girls," Kay said—this time with less concern and more annoyance.

The rest of the class seemed to know that already, and the girl, looking around to see if anyone else was as gagged as her, emitted a nervous laugh and let the class continue on learning how to learn *-ar* verbs in Spanish. It felt as if my biggest fear was playing out in front of my eyes, and then *boom:* nobody flinched, not even the girls who surely had been gossiping about it since we met Kay in the seventh grade. It wasn't an event; just a fact of attraction that Kay didn't have the desire to share with anybody until they had the gusto to ask. It's simple, the ways we other those who also have ownership of masculinity. Dressing masc automatically equaling a girl being gay also doesn't make sense.

I want to be pretty. In the same way that Black men want to be respected, never questioned, followed behind like a white woman starting a movement for her demographic and no one else. *Pretty* as in the softest form of me possible, a personality that is as silky as the shirts I now search for in thrift stores. I long for *pretty* so much that I volunteer at community thrift stores, spend hours looking in the deepest section of the '70s apparel, wishing somebody's dad dropped *pretty* off on his way to be something better. I long for every piece of myself that I didn't give to Gina, that I should've given to myself, that I should have given everyone around me in the years recovering from a loss, that I rejected during the years that happened before.

It didn't click for me that Gina and I were over for good until a phone call. I had moved away, bullied her into being in an open relationship, and called her up only to argue and get attention. When I wasn't getting the touch I wanted, and the San Marcos streets didn't desire what I dished out like I'd hoped, I called her up to say I would quit playing.

"It's been over for me for the past two months. You broke up with me. I gave up," she said. It was with the same matter-of-factness as Kay in that classroom. It was inevitable, my loss of her, her needing to get away from me, but that didn't mean I thought it would be now.

And it's true: I *did* break up with her. I always did with the subtext *it's not over* in my head, though I never said this out loud or in a way that made sense. Even in my best attempts to save this relationship—a familiar place, one where I failed to give her a hazmat suit when my toxicity inevitably came back—I could hear it in her voice. I could see through the phone that she was ready to be happy and heal from this unsettling experience. Even if I wanted to be happy, and with her, and get the help I overstood that I needed, I took too long to get my shit together. My cycle of abuse was no longer worth anything more than two sentences. Do you know how it feels to move from the center of someone's world to not even in their galaxy? I had to be with whatever ugliness I embraced alone. So then, finally, I went to therapy.

I moved from San Marcos to Forth Worth, and then to Austin, starting and stopping relationships at lightning speed. I reacquainted myself with men, their desires and needs, and remembered that I never was *enough.* I started to question where I ended up in this casualty; I reckoned with my years-long mistakes; I stopped blaming my actions on others. I mourned my friend in silence, in long cries in group therapy sessions, and in nights when someone's eyes weren't on me. I questioned what was *me,* what was the socialization of toxic masculinity, how I bought into the limited possibilities of "manhood."

And I'm here. Now, older. Less toxically masculine. Still questioning everything.

What I do know is that I want to be pretty. It took years for me to exonerate myself from my hands, make peace with Gina, and treat femmes in my life like humans—the antithesis of what was spoon-fed, mixed in with Gerber, to me. Even if I'm a good person, and haven't lifted my voice/hand to anyone since Gina, I write this essay detailing every manly thing I've ever done. Even if I spent years scared of what I was capable of when brought down by depression and afraid; even if I was canceled, then able to build myself back up, masculinity is me. I can't say that every display of it has been good.

I can't say that when I see the word "masculine" online, or uttered by some men and masc people, it doesn't give me "ick," but I can say that the tearing up of myself and everyone else around me, for me, has stopped. For years, I was not worthy of a Gina, a Kay, a love at all if I couldn't learn to open myself up and grow. I could wish I never did the things I did, or I could admit to them and let history un-repeat itself. Nobody can punish me more than what the world already does to Black men, butches, studs, transmasculine people, so why not be honest? Why not use this time we have in these bodies to be better?

These days, I have new outlooks on Black masculinity. My masculinity means confidence, daring to question toxicity, wearing prettiness in a world that sees us as aggressive by default. It means honesty; I'm honestly into telling femmes who I was and who I strive to be; I don't ask for help when I won't help myself. I am myself, not a template of masculinity that's come before; just myself. I am that hellish teenage nightmare letting history fall all over me and deciding to wash it off as I dip myself into perception that isn't seen as pretty. My past is singed to me, housed in my heart as a reminder when I'm quick to judge Black masc people for something they shouldn't be doing.

We can shed ourselves, be limitless, and embody everything *pretty.* I am mine, you are yours, this world is ours, everyone's, to be safe in.

Even if the world treats us as obsolete, we still need
each other. Fetch me tea that helps me shit properly—
feel my stomach cave in on itself when I tell you
the hardest thing I have to admit. I want to hug
instead of hurt, tell my mother I'm sorry and un-own
anything that makes me harden. The moon is most
moon when we look up to see it. I look up and past
my mess to see a better me, swinging on the moon.
I'm in my prettiest silk shirt and singing down to myself:
how does it feel, to be free?

I'm Not FTM. I Am

person2insect
insect2lemur
lemur2tap shoe
tap shoe2emo
emo2pornstar
pornstar2guitar
guitar2croon
croon2Jazmine Sullivan
silky Jazmine vocals2bed sheet
bed sheet2sheetrock
sheetrock2ocean
ocean2poet
poet2pessimist
pessimist2activist
activist2jail cell
jail cell2phone line
phone line2picket sign
picket sign2loss of life
Loss2laughing; remembering
Laughing; remembering2flower;
flower2adderall
adderall2person
person2tree
andgrowing—

How I Learned to Love My Chest

We all enter this place with a body. Skinny, fat, tall, short, freckled, and all the beauty in between those man-made identifiers. We all enter this place with a physical form that tethers us to the ground, somehow. I can't remember a time when the body I was born with wasn't a perpetual "before" in the "before and after" pictures in those posts people put on social media when they've lost weight. I can't remember a time I looked in the mirror and didn't say—in my head, heart, or out loud—"this will change one day." I can't remember when, but sometime overnight when I was ten, my chest went from flat as the ground we're all tethered to, to as round as the earth's figure. It confused me, and I'd found another thing to factor into my "before" pic.

Since they started to grow in, my boobs were a point of contention for me. I've never entered a room and been perceived as small—not only cause my body takes up space needed for it to move, but also this essence, this energy that tells passersby that I'm some kind of queer—so when I grew breasts larger than all my classmates', it made the problem—being a fat, butch, Black girl—more metastasized.

My boobs always felt too big, too present, too much of a giveaway that I was a "girl." My training bras couldn't hold up all this difference. It didn't help that I was clocked as butch; if anyone wanted to bully me, they could easily talk about the juxtaposition between the clothes I wore—ripped jeans, Vans or Nikes, and fitted caps—and the giant knockers that sat plump on my chest.

"Why are they like that?" they'd say. Embarrassment was colored all over my face like crayons every day of grade school. Around thirteen, I started to need double-D bras to keep them upright. So many days, I wore two bras just so I would get fewer comments from peers about how gravity naturally pulled them down.

How could I give the flesh I didn't want back to where it came from? It was horrible, to all of a sudden get unwanted attention.

Being the fat, Black "he-she" in middle school was like being a billboard visible on the side of the highway that reads DON'T DATE ME. While all the kids around me were doing the things people in the hood do in middle school—getting boyfriends, trying weed, having their first kisses, and the like—I was making high A's on all my tests and going home straight after school. In a sea of Black kids that were just as poor and broken as me, nobody wanted to hang out. Nobody wanted to be as "weird" and fat as me. No boy wanted to switch IDs and put 'em around our necks to soft-launch our relationship. I was the girl that gave off boyfriend energy. If I was ever a girl, I was only one when people saw my chest. My hips and chub added insult to injury.

Life felt like hell, and I must've been the person guarding the restrooms there. I knew I had to do something different.

Cause we live in a limit-filled world, the main identifier for my forthcoming womanhood was my chest. Even when I was in "women's" clothes, folks acted like they couldn't tell I was a girl until they walked right up on me. When I started having sex, my natural reflex was to cover or hide my chest so no one would look, no matter the gender of the lover.

"Why do you do that?" partners upon partners said post-coitus. I didn't really have a reason that I wasn't ashamed to speak, so what usually came out in response was some variation of "Cause." Often, I also changed the subject. It's hard to feel like the body that you want and the body that you need are not aligned, especially when you don't have honest examples of transness in your world.

I learned to hate myself before I learned love that transcends our sacks of bone and blood; it showed in all the ways that I shrunk myself. First, in friendships, denying myself of all their hugs. Second, in pictures, only taking them from the top of my chest up in earlier days of Instagram. Third, in romance; every girl I dated knew not to hug me too close, nor expect me to take off my shirt during sex. I learned to distance love from this body that I didn't want.

And I mastered this art, this living in loss and without, while imagining my best self in another dimension. I didn't know that I could do anything but be ashamed—that is, not until I was marketed something on Instagram years later.

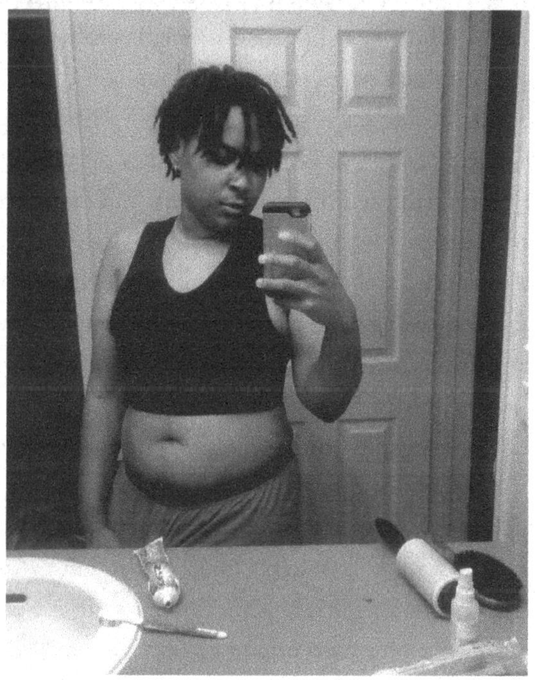

My first picture in a binder, circa 2019

"Yo! Here's me trying on a binder," I said in a shaky video. The year was 2018. I was scrolling aimlessly and came across some trans influencer doing a marketing deal with a brand. The guy was doing a try-on of some kind of contraption that looked like a bra, but instead of holding your tits up, the contraption compressed them down in an effort to make your chest appear flat, thus eliminating giggles from strangers indefinitely. I looked at what his chest looked like before and after using the binder and was amazed; in T-minus 30 seconds, this guy with a B- or C-cup chest became completely flat. You wouldn't even know he had boobs if not for the video itself! I *had* to have this thing.

He also mentioned that there were other brands, but this one was his favorite. There were multiple brands providing this mystery product?!?! A whole world opened to me. I scrolled and scrolled through the products pages of multiple brands—TransTape, gc2b, UNTAG, FLAVNT, etc.—to find a brand who'd intentionally put up pictures of models with bigger bodies. I perused YouTube for people who had tried different binders, and discovered that it wasn't just trans guys who used these things. Transmascs, butches, and cosplayers needed binders too! Eventually, I landed on just trying a brand and seeing what happened. I paid my fifty dollars and waited, impatiently, on my new portal into life for two weeks.

The package of my two new binders came, and immediately I dropped everything to try one on. In the mirror of my bathroom, I wiggled a small binder over my head, did some readjusting to make my heavy boobs fit under it, then turned sideways in the mirror. I fell in love with what I saw. It wasn't completely flat, but flatter than I'd ever seen my post-puberty self. It was the moment my endorphins started flirting with my perception of pain. It was as if I was transported back to that flat-chested ten-year-old I once was. I looked in the mirror and felt more than indifferent about what I saw. I put on a shirt and fell more in love with my new and improved body. It was the closest thing I'd felt to self-love.

So yes, I recorded a cheesy little video displaying my excitement for my Instagram Stories viewers. I watched the comments immediately flood in.

"This is the happiest I've seen you in years," a close friend said.

"Looking good! Should I say handsome, or—" another friend quipped. I could feel a confidence long lost come flooding back into my body. At the time, I'd just started identifying as nonbinary; surely, I thought, this would stop people from mis-pronouning* me. Sure, my double-Ds lumped under the compression of the skin-tight nylon and spandex. Sure, I only had money to buy two, and I couldn't wear them for more than twelve hours straight. I didn't care, cause I had finally found LOVE. There was at least one thing I could hide about my body more effectively.

I have to celebrate, I thought. The beginning of the rest of my life had just started. This was a cause for a fancy meal (on a budget), so I went to a semi-expensive sushi spot in my vicinity, ready to be finally seen as who I am.

"Hey! Welcome to ____________. How may I help you?" the smiley waiter asked.

"Yo! For now, I'd like a water with a lime."

"For sure! Would you like any appetizers or cocktails to start you out?"

"I need a couple more minutes to look at the menu."

"Right on. I'll be back in a minute with your water. If there's anything else you need, ma'am, my name is [blank] and I'll be your

* I use this term instead of "misgender." See more info about this choice here: https://hunterthelion.medium.com/you-could-never-misgender-me-d5e9687d8523.

server for tonight." Just like that, I was slapped back into reality. This binder wasn't holding back shit.

It's not that I thought I would be he/him'd or anything. After all, my voice was still high, and we don't live in a world where people don't immediately assign a gender to you the moment they perceive your body. I at least thought, though, that people would pause longer, but no; I didn't change enough for the she/hers to stop raining in on me. My binder didn't put up enough of a fight against centuries of gender initiation; gender segregation; gendered violence; I got an appetizer and an entrée to go. I cried into my bed as comments continued to tell me I looked good, happy, finally at peace with this flesh. I cried cause I thought I'd done enough.

For months, I intentionally wore the binder too long, I forced it off me and hushed my redness to sleep with gentle strokes across my flesh. In a way, this felt like the most tender I'd ever been with myself. During sex with women ready to see all of me, I would keep the binder on, close my eyes, and imagine myself as the boy I'd seen in my daydreams. When the deed was done, I shamefully went to the restroom to take off the sweat-filled binder; of course, they functioned as glorified bras after a number of stretches and pulls.

I wanted so badly to make binding work. I wanted to have an eternal fix for my years-long problem of having breast tissue. I knew that top surgery was an option, but I'd gone through hell just coming out as queer years prior, so I didn't want another reason for people I loved to treat me like shit.

I cried that night, the first night I came home from binding, cause I knew what I eventually had to do next.

A couple of weeks before my top surgery, I was still crowdfunding for the cost. Luckily, I'd gotten a full-time job with benefits months prior, so I didn't have to come off ten thousand–plus dollars like my transmasc siblings with no insurance. Still, when factoring in miscellaneous costs—travel to and from the doctor, supplies, medicine I needed for recovery time, food, and the deductible I still had to pay—I needed about three thousand dollars to make it. This wasn't something most Black twenty-four-year-olds without trust funds or family to lean on have. I had a full-time job that paid the most I'd ever been paid, which was $45,000 a year (read: *not enough to have money saved up when you live in Austin, Texas*).

My initial crowdfunding plan was to host a variety show. I was over using GoFundMe and Facebook donations for fundraisers—it felt so dehumanizing to do—and I'd been putting on shows in my city for some time. I luckily had built up my contacts with comics, musicians, and poets, and I'd found both a venue willing to donate the space and local businesses willing to donate products that I could then auction off. It was gonna be a *function,* honey! But it was planned for April 2020, and we all know how that went. I was then stuck crowdfunding on social media—arguably the most demeaning way to crowdfund in this day and age—and though I was close to my goal amount, I was feeling pretty defeated. On my last leg of hope, I sent individual texts to everyone in my phone asking if they could help me get over the final hump, or if they could repost my stuff on socials so that I could reach monied people. Most didn't reply (typical), but some did, one of which I'll never forget.

"Who is this?" the white guy I'd done a couple low-paying shows with in the past said.

"It's KB! Sorry; we haven't talked for a minute, but I thought you'd be interested in helping me out with this."

"Oh yeah, hey! I hope you're doing well. I really want you to reconsider this. I've just heard of too many people regretting it once it's done and you are a really pretty girl and I don't want you to do something irreversible for what may give you temporary joy. I care about your long-term well-being /:"

Mind you, this man didn't know who I was thirty seconds ago. Now all of a sudden he cares about my "long-term well-being" with a slash face. I looked and looked at this text.

I looked, first searching for where the logic might emerge, wondering if I should send something snarky in response or just let him live within this country-mandated delusion. In all my childhood daydreams, I was the "boy." Cause boy-girl depictions were the only thing I saw on TV screens as a kid, I had to be one, and I couldn't be the girl since I'd never pictured myself in the things that girls wore. In rom-coms and fairy tales, the girl was always thin, non-Black, wearing dresses, heels, and skirts, always wanting the touch of a man so bad, you could see it in her (sometimes animated) bones.

What does it feel like, to have somebody waiting their whole life for you, I wondered. The only way I could find out was to be the man that the beautiful woman wanted. All I had to do was lose a few pounds, take the gym more seriously so I could gain a V-cut, and find something to do with my chest. *That* is what I believed for decades, and I tried hard to not be myself in real life because of some stranger cishet white boys like this.

Instead of sending him the litany of texts cussing him out that he deserved, I left his message on read, and continued to text my actual friends.

You ever listened to Solange's *When I Get Home* and really got in your body? You ever been at home alone, in an apartment complex that don't got your A/C on or your best interest at heart, and your neighbors noisy as hell so you know they wouldn't hear you, and used your bite-sized, cheap Bluetooth speaker to blast that whole album back-to-back? You ever had a hard year and needed to bury it in the spirit of Houston and harmonies you can't guess upon first listen, and smokey instruments that feel like they're being played for the backdrop of your life? Have the spirit of confusion and wine ever entered your body at the same time?

Have you ever mixed together headache-inducing, twenty-dollar red wine and sadness and had to numb yourself to the body you never got to know in the first place? You ever been naked in front of no one but yourself; you ever wanted nakedness so badly but never been alone long enough to have it? You ever told yourself how you really feel about *it*? You ever spent your whole childhood alone, then lived an adulthood that's more sadness-to-sadness than anything? You ever played catch-up with touch? You ever spent hours on social media posts just scrolling till your eyes say *stop* and still scrolling after that to find something that makes you feel touch?

You know what touch is—the feeling of fingerprints on your thigh and neck and face and genitals? The feeling of someone asking you if you're okay, have you eaten today, did you eat before drinking all this wine, do you want to hug for no reason? Have you ever been somewhere that tells your body you're in paradise? A beach that has just enough sunlight and the water temperature is perfect? A street where nothing stands in between you and where you're trying to go, where time isn't of the essence at all? You ever had company over that you didn't know well, and questioned your sense of reality, and did every bad thing you ever read in one of those stories with a clear villain, and your body tensed up/told you to stop grinding your teeth/told you you're not being yourself, and you wanted to cum more than you wanted to listen to your body? Has your body ever felt like *you*? Has your body ever been more than a dumping ground, a conduit, a conglomerate of food you need to eat to live and eat to feel some kind of endorphin you're not feeling otherwise?

Have you gotten joy from anything other than food and false connection? You ever run away from yourself so long that you don't know what's on your chest? Is it big thoughts, or big boobs, or both—you ever questioned your gender so long that you don't know what the question is? Have you thought that being alone is too much like death since you died a million times over the past ten years? You ever have a vein flare up and your throat clench and your back strain cause you were too close to alone and naked and touch? You ever flinch cause a lover of the night or a lifetime wanted to touch your chest? You ever been alone and listened to Solange's *When I Get Home*? Last time I did, I emailed a top surgeon's office from my phone and said fuck it let's do this—

On April 23, 2020, in the belly of a health crisis I'd never seen before, fourteen years after knowing that I had a chest, two years into binding until I gave myself bloody rashes, one month into the only relationship where I've let a partner touch my chest, I got a life-affirming procedure known as top surgery. If I could accurately describe the moment endorphins have gay sex with your pain and turn it into sustained pleasure and happiness, the moments I've lived in my body since top surgery have felt like that. When I was able to write during the week of recovery, I wrote a laundry list of ways I could love myself better, and all the things I would do now that I'd gotten something off my chest (haha).

"Look at yourself in the mirror more" and "dance like nobody's watching every time you dance," I wrote, softly, to myself. Though I'm still working on self-love, I am more naked and free to touch myself and others than I've ever been.

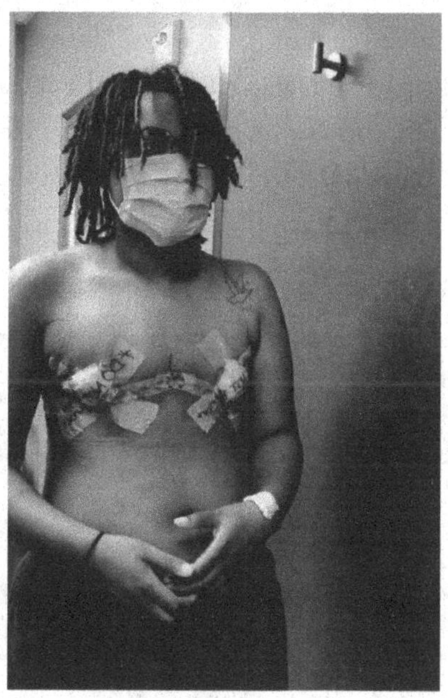

Me, shirtless, one week after top surgery, 2020

When I say "earned touch," I don't mean that anyone should have to work as hard and long as I did to feel worthy of nakedness. No one in this world deserves to feel distant from their body, or like they don't know what love is, for any era or time in their lives. One day, we will realize that the archaic ways we view people and their bodies don't work for anybody; until then, I'm telling you the story of how I learned to love myself and to know that I deserve touch.

Now, I touch myself all the time—too much, even. I touch myself when I swim shirtless in the pool, and when I am alone and dancing till my skin is damp with joy. I could talk about the two large scars that appear on my body post-op, or how I'm still fat and undesired by some cause of it, or how I have sex without clothes now, or how my partner makes me feel like the cutest person on this side of the South, but maybe those are other pieces; this piece is about how, since we don't live in a world where touch is offered to people with bodies and gender variance like me, I learned to love myself.

Picture of me riding a bike for the first time in ten years, and riding a bike shirtless for the first time ever, circa 2021

I want every person with a body to feel the way I've felt since April 23, 2020. I hope to live long enough to forget there was a "before" this. I want my new scars to outlive the extra flesh that was there before them; I believe that every person is owed healthcare, and specifically healthcare that will help them be mentally, spiritually, and physically sound. That includes top surgery, bottom surgery, HRT, facial feminization, abortions paid for by the state, mental healthcare paid for by the state, and any other medicine or procedure necessary for a person's overall health. I believe we should live in times that our country wants everyone to live in. This is a wish as well as a manifestation. One day, in my lifetime, or in a timeline that succeeds me, in some time that trans people inevitably will exist in, everyone will be treated as someone. And this, my friend, won't require a coming-out.

Sonnet Five

There is a fruit the hue of ketchup. The fruit
dangles from my evergreen childhood tree.
Botanists call it Juniper. I see it
& my mind automatically taints leaves
with the chasm of memory. Again
proceeds the exploding structure of epithets;
once more, the rupture of language
overheard from the lips a love-lost man.
I hid behind a tree. My father called me
anything but the name of god. Now I am
a figment of fissures spilling out
from Jupiter, a quiet May noon's
sinister background. How cruel, queer nature's breeze.
Little ants and honeybees will carry my casket.

I Get Least of You

Dad,

I can see exactly how you look as I'm writing this letter. Slumped over reading a Bible at 2 a.m., prepping for a sermon at the church everyone thinks is yours. Your skin has tiny holes where hair and non-clogged pores used to be. There is soda, catfish, and any meat you can ingest in that fauz-beer belly. You are the Texas man that went outta style after cowboy Westerns and chaining up dogs outside did. You have brown, coarse hands that are the closest to the same hue on both sides that I've ever seen. These are the hands I was afraid of when Mama said to stop poppin' my knuckles. You likely just looked up at me from the corner of your brown reading glasses, wondering what I need in the kitchen this late.

When I was young, I understood myself to be the daughter you and my mama always wanted. If you let Granny tell it, you let me be a complete brat, and I got everything that I wanted cause of it. I understood that I needed to exist in ways that were comfortable for you—the head of our household—in order to have an excess of love in this life.

But then, I turned ten.

Puberty came, and I sweated through every night. Our drippy old A/C tended to not circulate past the den, and my room was always five degrees hotter than the rest of the house. I had too much blubber to make it through eight hours unconscious without getting drippy with sweat, and you loved to tell me losing weight would stop that. It was this summer, the summer before sixth grade, that you started to love me less.

One of those sweaty nights, our church's pastor called to ask if I was gay. You asked Mama, and Mama asked you. Nervous with slobber dried up on my mouth, I said something like:

"If I was, why does it matter?" This was after every damn classmate asked and I vehemently denied it, and after twelve years of reinforcement from everybody in the family/school/churches I encountered that being gay was asking for death. I was tired of the question, frankly, and tired of everyone never answering my simple question—*why does it matter*—before getting inquisitive about me.

You wouldn't look me in the face the rest of that year.

Another night, I had a "church friend" over. Lyriq was older, more mischievous, and insisted on introducing me to things I shouldn't have known about for years. Mama caught us doing one of the many things we weren't supposed to do—the terrible thing, the *gay* thing—and we both got the worst whoopin' of our lives. It is after this moment that I knew you wouldn't love me the same ever again.

I would've loved to have a protector when the church started to do wrong by me. I needed your love to not come with the condition that I would perform girlhood how you imagined it when you told my bio-granny "I've always wanted a girl." Having expectations of a child—like them cleaning up their room and being honest—are valid, but having expectations that a child be the fantasy you wanted is not right, nor was it consensual for me. You and other parents should adjust your expectations once children develop their own personalities and desires. I wanted to say this to you before now, but I haven't.

At twenty-one, seven years after I freed myself from your church, I started to question everything even more than I already was. Once I was outside the confines of our six blocks of Fort Worth, I explored what it meant to be a queer person while not under the nose of you and other nearby relatives. In an Afam Lit class, I watched this two-hour dialogue between James Baldwin and Nikki Giovanni from the 1971 show *Soul!* by Ellis Haizlip. The year you were twenty-one, they were talking about stuff I wished I was able to say to you. Giovanni said something I felt the moment I laid eyes on you before I left Fort Worth for good:

> *Why you gon' be truthful with me when you lie to everybody else? You lied when you smiled at that cracker down at the job, right? Lie to me; smile; treat me the same way you would treat him. You must! You must, cause I've caught the frowns and the anger. He's happy with you; of course he doesn't know you're unhappy. You grin at him all day long. You come home and I catch hell cause I love you. I get least of you. I get the very minimum. And I'm saying, fake it with me. Is that too much of the Black woman to ask of the Black man?*

There is so much to be said about how addiction has ravaged the Black community—you manifest this through your use of cigarettes, power, and misdirected rage. There is so much to be said about the pressure of being a Black man—the main source of income for the nuclear household, a source of income for grandkids, the main punching bag for a company you gave forty-five years to, and—for better or worse—the final decision-maker for multiple different people's decisions. In our house, you spoke for me, my mother, and yourself, without us asking you to. There's so much to be said about having your source of stability—driving that Sears van from town to town—taken away due to ageism and capitalism's necessity for bodies that have years of wear and tear left on them. There's no other way that laying you off made sense, since you knew the ins and outs of every washing and drying machine that's ever existed, and you had enough qualifications to be running the place. The fights that we had felt less about my individual fuck-ups and more about your disgruntlement with your position in the world.

When I could see through the tears in my eyes while you lashed me with a belt or a switch, it was as if you weren't there. You were just a vessel, using a child to channel what you wished you could've done into your circumstances. So many things negatively affected you and, in return, our experience together. To add insult to injury, I could not live up to your desires, your precious little girl. I was the bearer of bad news every day that I existed around you. It was and is . . . heavy.

Partially I think that our issues are due to your lack of education and my lack of patience. I remember times when Mama would just ask me to show her how to do something on a smartphone so both you boomers knew how to work them. I would be so annoyed that I'd blow off the conversation entirely. I was annoyed with Mama and especially you all through high school. Now I wish that I didn't do that, that I trusted you more to absorb new information about me, but what can I say; me coming out wasn't quite well received, so I went into myself, like you. In that way, I am my father's daughter.

Now you only call me on accident. Now, you appear in the background of my phone calls with Mama, who is losing her memory by the day. Now there is so much unsaid, and I've created enough walls to build houses between us. You built houses in yourself better than you built up washing and drying machines.

Half of this is both our faults, and half of that is what white supremacy has done to us. Dad, I wish that I could still be your little prized possession and bring back the times we had when I was your girl. But when I see images of little kids, adult kids, adolescent kids and their fathers, it used to make me want more between us. Now I've lived more life without you than with you. Now I've accepted that I've gotten least of you.

From my perspective, you spent my childhood being good to everyone else—the cashier at the local grocery store that doesn't think of you once you leave the building, my cousins and extended family that only call when they need a washer fixed; everyone, Dad. You are the spark, the man with the meaty, beautiful voice that sings nothing but church songs. To them, you are the voice that swims even when your lungs swim in lakes of smoke. I got least of you, always.

Twenty-seven years. We've been in each other's lives for twenty-seven years—fifteen of those years under the same roof. Out of those fifteen years, five of them left me feeling feral, dadless, purposeless to you. Everyone thinks highly of you cause the fake self, the mask that you take with you when you leave the house, is the life of the party. Outside of our house on Radford Road, one of your selves is a comedian. The honest one, the one that me and Mama know, is addicted to cigarettes and power over your household and wife. The one I fell in love with was the sweet man who *chose* to be my father. I've seen him in photo albums; I remember him in small flickers; I wish I knew more of him than *him.*

Still, I want to believe we can repair this. I wanna believe in everybody's capacity to do better, really. I want to believe that when I come back to town in a couple of weeks, something good will happen when I come out as trans, though I'm prepared for it to go poorly. I want to believe that something will make my hope feel less unfounded. I want to believe in you, Dad. The only dad I've ever seen with my eyes can't be a lost cause.

Dad, I think I have too much weary for a person my age. It's gotten thick; hard; ashy as a tortoiseshell; outside of which I was your girl at ten. I don't cry, and when I do, my body has an involuntary reflex that makes my tear ducts shrivel up and reverse. I want to blame that on my HRT, but really, it is my weary. I've had my addictions since ten—porn, social media, feeling important—and I've had my violent run-ins with power, like you. They're different from yours but still present. They made my body crave death more, so I had to stop it. I know you can stop it.

I see too much of you in me—the man I am assumed to be. I'm trying to heal from things, and I hope that there's a sliver of a chance that you'd be open to trying alongside me. I want to have a conversation about what we've known since I was ten: I'm not a girl, and I tried my hardest for years to be your girl, to get your love back, but I can't pretend like when you say "she" in reference to me it doesn't feel like you're talking about somebody else. I wish it felt like you were berating somebody else—all those years I spent hating you as a teen. I can't continue to answer to a name that hasn't existed in my social circles for at least three years; I can't continue to believe that you don't know that who you want me to be never existed. Some people say that they were born trans. I think I was born unable to *girl* in the way you've wanted me to. I wasn't born attached to a gender. Just, like everyone, wanting to be loved.

I feel the same as you about manhood now, Dad. I wish I had someone with years of understanding about what it means to live in this Black manhood I've inherited. It's manhood, meaning *madness.* I wish we could have conversations about this—though "he/him" is not my ministry, it is my perception and therefore also my problem. I accept that, and want to be part of the solution.

I think I got least of you cause the world's shunned almost all of you Black boys and chipped away at what you could've been. I know you had dreams before you were a worker, Dad; I've seen the basketball championship pictures.

These past two years—ones where I've been perceived by the gender-ignorant eye as a Black man—have been the hardest, most traumatizing years of my life. I can't begin to think about what seventy-one years of this have been like for you. It must've been hard to mourn that girl—who turned into a never-existing woman—the girl you thought would soften you.

And that is a problem. Too many men wait until they have daughters to care about women. Too many men, including you, dish out love with unfair conditions. "I love you, only if ____________." Love with a "PS: be my girl" attached to it ain't love at all. A girl shouldn't have to be your daughter, or lover, or lover that is subservient to you, in order to feel loved.

I wish I had contact with my bio-dad; that's not to say you didn't do the best job that you could've. But I think that there is something significant about blood. I'd love to know where both sides of this trauma come from, and I'd love to be able to sit down with both of you. What does it mean to parent yourself in a world that sees you as a man while you are a boy? What does it mean to be told that you're a boy—like I was told that I was a girl—and have Blackness cloak that boy in some predetermined fate? I was never a Black boy, but now I'm expected to be a Black man. I'd love to get the MO on all I missed from boyhood with you and dad #2.

I miss you. Or at least I miss the you that was a sweet man.

Dad,

I can see you now with your blond-dyed, multiple-sized locs tied up in a bun. Your round face, burgeoning prickly black mustache, caramel brown (depending on the time of year) skin, and peeling pink lips. I see your silver necklace, your belly you can see before you see your feet when looking down, your scarred-up legs and arms, your hairy back and chest, your shitty tattoos, hazel eyes, and million-dollar smile. You are somewhere in me so I figure you look exactly like me, too. I'm looking in the mirror right now, knowing I look like someone that has existed.

In my mind, I know that if we ever met, I'd look like you, since I don't look like my bio-mom or bio-granny or anybody else on that side of the family. Besides the thick thighs (which have saved heat and not lives), I have nothing that traces me back to my bio-mom's side. I figure we'd have a lot to say to each other, so I'm writing this letter to you as a head start. Who wants a years-long synopsis of a late twentysomething's life story, anyway?*

It is my hope that, through 23andMe, or some prison registry, or some death certificate, I can get closer to you and all living relatives you may have. Though I doubt a lot of niggas are using 23andMe, I've heard from other people that have used it that they tell you if your DNA is similar enough to other people that have used it, so I figure I can at least try it out. If not, I don't think I'll be heartbroken since I've lived twenty-seven years without you, but I want to get this off my chest: I hope you're somewhere wondering in some way about your legacy.

If you are around the age of Bio-mama you'd be a forty-five-year-old Black man/woman/soul. Many folk at this age are wondering what it means to be Black and middle-aged, since there isn't a lot of guidance on it; aging resources are painfully white. If you're somewhere Black and beautiful like I think you are, I hope you're thinking of what it is that you contributed to the world during your time on this big, green, conflicted-ass earth.

Let me tell you a little about me.

I'm a survivor of childhood sexual assault, anti-Black racism, gender dysphoria and stress, the K–12 school system in Texas,

* You, I assume. <3

chronic pain, classism, and mental illnesses. Since you're in the Black skin I'm in too, you may be able to guess that many things were set up for me to fail in these twenty-seven years of life. I've dropped out of school twice, but I have won enough awards for them to take up a page of my CV. I've been excommunicated from friend groups, but I've written two books—this one being my third. I also have a barrack of people who love me enough to go to war if needed, and a godson who's doing well in his first year of school, and a partner who is everything more than anything I've imagined. Bio-mama is alive, well, and doing much-anticipated repair with me and herself. For what it's worth, I'm in the best position of this fucked-up, unconsented journey we call life. Though it's been a hard one, it's been a life, and for that, I'm grateful to you.

I don't know what your relationship with Mama was like, but I do know that she was in the worst era of her life when I was conceived. After years of ridicule and abuse, she turned to the only thing she knew to turn to—all the things that the other kids in the hood turned to—sex. It could've been drugs, or suicide, so I'm grateful it made me. I've been a miracle question ever since. While sitting down at a coffee shop, I asked a bio-mom question I've been too scared to ask—"Who is my dad?"—for the second time, and she looked me in the face with the most worried look I've ever seen in any eyes, and said, "I don't know."

Dad, I've been dreaming of you since I was two.

There are so many different scenarios that I made up about how our meeting might go. You have so many different faces, levels of facial hair, senses of style, types of haircuts, interests, jobs. Bio-mama said she had "an idea" of who you might be, but it would be cruel to share since it could be wrong. I agree with her, kind of. Are you the person she suspects, or someone else? Whoever you are, I hope that you're a good person.

I don't know your current gender, but I know you'd been a Black man for at least eighteen years when Bio-mom knew you. Maybe you could tell me a thing or two about what it means. I've been needing guidance real bad, Dad. If we ever met, I'd likely start the sentence with something like "Fuck." Did I get my sailor mouth from you? I figure, since I'm grown as hell, you wouldn't mind that justified reaction, but I wonder if you're the "my children can never cuss in my presence" type. I'd like to think you'd excuse me anyway.

There's something to be said about the fact that I would not be surprised if I found you through a prison registry. Or a sex-offender list, or a death certificate. Based on the flagrant ways that my safety has been compromised just in the past year, I figure that this life has caused you some damage. It's safe to say that not having you in my life has caused me some damage as well—mostly internal struggle when people talk about looking like their dad. And having a good relationship with their dad. And knowing their dad's name, age, face—the like. The guy that I call Dad now did the best that he knew how with the broken tools he had, probably. And he chose to be my dad during his youngest son's battle with cancer. A man, if there ever was one.

Seeing a Black boy you raised die before your eyes, and still choosing to commit to sixteen years of my life, is admirable. A best friend of mine died in 2016, and I don't think I'll ever recover, Dad. I wonder sometimes if you are my current dad's deceased son—since everyone thought I was his brother's son, until a paternity test proved otherwise. Did my mother find love with you? Was I just a mistake to you?

My adopted parents started raising me when I was two. I wonder how different life would have been if I knew you, or if you met me then. A less-evolved version of me wrote a poem about Bio-mom that was scathing. I don't stand by it anymore, but it was a poem

I needed to write with the limited information I could find about you: nothing. I wrote because I was upset about that *nothing.* Bio-mom texted me after she read my mean-ass poem, saying something like "giving you away was the hardest decision ever." I'd like to think that not knowing you was my hardest decision, a decision I never chose. I forgive her and you both.

I'll be honest. I haven't put in any effort past one question—*Who is my dad?*—to find you until now; I think it's cause not finding you after actually trying would've crushed me before I turned twenty-seven. The world already was crushing me, so I can handle it. All the things I've been through have hardened me so, so much; without the work of therapy and love, I'd be hunched over, hating you and Bio-mom forever. I'm ready to write this letter to you, and then send a box of my DNA to 23andMe, and, if that doesn't work out, maybe entertain one or two other avenues.

I know we don't know each other, but I do love you. You collabed to make my breath and blood possible. You made my words, these words, that have reached so many possible. I can't deny that.

These days, I spend most of my days writing poems and essays to strangers. This is as much a letter for me as it is for you. If my manifesting powers are worth any fucking thing, you'll see this, and in another cosmic world, I'll meet you and you'll meet dad #1 before death meets him. I'd love for us, three generations of perceived-Black men, to talk about how we can be better people, to multiply what we give to each other. I may have gotten least of you, but I believe you can give more, Dad. I haven't cried in something like a year, but I would allow myself to if I met you.

Who knows, maybe we've already met. If it's less than 1 percent of a possibility, then that means it could've happened to me. I'm Black, trans, and alive; those odds are terrible. I've gone on many plane rides, talked to many audiences, turned my fuckups into sentences that bring people joy more times than I was allowed; *anything* is possible, Dad. If you introduced yourself as anyone other than my dad, I wouldn't know who you are. All this hate I should have, given how awful the world has been, and still, I have love to give. Isn't that something? Everyone in our life is a stranger until they aren't. The only thing that tethers us is blood.

And location. And lust, love, and the internet. I am always dramatic. I want to be a better person, and I hope we have that in common, stranger. I wonder if you have other children, if they have children and aunties, uncles, niblings, people I'm destined to love. I'm ready to expand my barrack of love, and I hope you'll join me in it. I wish I could tell you more, but I have to go back to work. I got least of you due to human circumstances, and I'm finally ready to forgive the universe for it. I want more of myself, and that means I want more of you. I'm trying to have fewer questions without answers in my life as I grow into somebody's Black man.

Miss you. Or at least the person I hope for.

Dads,

When the world wanted the most of you both, I wanted the very least. Just presence, kindness, never commenting on my weight, always protecting me from ______, teaching me how to be a person I need. When the pastor you thought was your friend asked you if I was queer, I needed you. When other kids had dads, happy to be with them at open houses, I needed you. I needed you like I need a needle and blood to inject T into. I need calls to get to both of you, or at least, sometimes I think I do.

Miss you. Or at least I miss most of you.

With love,

KB

I'm trying to see some things, feel some things, be some things he couldn't

Often, we stone mothers,
make them make sense of why our dads hold us at far
distances, interesting how a ho never reaches so far
as to bar herself from fatal fate—

craving ache, Black boys take centuries to discover themselves,
ask for help, get out of jail; hell is hell-bent
on Black men & men are hell-bent on running
from sense. Picture me, being myself,

not helping them throw me into depths
of a grave, eating shades of sunlight, beating
Hades allegations with my actions, so upright,
so in line with my values—loving god, feeding
the god in me. My people are sandwiched between

this realm and the next one, begging
everyone lusting for our blood to snap out of it.
For my ancestors, just finally, snap out of it—

23andMe

I thought about it for years. Since the day in high school when I sent my birth mom a text, saying, simply:

"Who is my dad?"

I thought about it in the thirty minutes she took to respond. The people I'd lived with since I was two years old weren't my blood-parents. I knew that since elementary school, but the need to know more, to fill the missing slot that was "birth dad," didn't come till I was probably thirteen. That was the age when the question mark around half of my genes started to feel like a knife.

"I don't know, baby . . . I'm sorry," my birth mom said in response to my question.

It must've felt out of the blue for her, but she *had* to know I would ask eventually. I convinced myself that her answer was enough, that the period at the end of her sentence was the end of my father-finding journey, but of course I thought about it for years.

Who did I get my eyes from? My nose? All the features that I couldn't find in my birth mom's bloodline? Then, twelve years later, the boss at my first grown-up job mentioned that they'd had a sibling they never knew existed. They learned this information through 23andMe.

"It was WILD," they said with wide eyes, explaining how shocked their parents were that they found out. "It happened when my dad was really young. Me and my sister's first phone call lasted hours." And then, some decades-old questions came tumbling to the front of my brain. What if I also had secret siblings? Like with many things from childhood, I'd buried the fact that I asked my birth mom about my dad, but at this moment, I thought about it again.

I had to at least do more. I at least had to try to get some consolation for the fact that I'd had to learn from a deficit of knowing what made me, I thought. So I opened Google and searched:

"Will 23andMe help me find a parent?"

I bought a kit. I tried to stay patient while it came to me.

"Hey M! This is [deadname] (I go by KB though). I live in Austin and just got my 23andMe results. I'm trying to find one of my parents. Let me know if you'd be down to connect! My number is ______. Thank you." Weeks before I sent this message to a stranger, my 23andMe kit came in and I sent loads of spit to some faraway lab full of more strangers. Later, I got an email saying I had access to view my ancestry, traits, and a bevy of DNA Relatives from across the globe.

Whew, I beat the white dad allegations, I thought, chuckling. According to 23andMe, I am 88.7% sub-Saharan African. It was a running joke amongst some less-than-kind peers in middle school that I had a white dad since my eyes were so light. Though that was, of course, ignorant of them to say, I felt vindicated with this newly verified information. If my dad is any kind of white, it's less than 8%; saying I was white would be like those white people who claim to be one-tenth Cherokee or whatever.

When I initially looked up "Will 23andMe help me find a parent?," their website said that their services weren't designed for this, and at best, I could expect some relatives that were generations removed. *But my boss found a sibling,* I thought. *I have to at least try.* As expected, almost all my DNA Relatives were four or more generations away. But one.

Just one person had more than 23% DNA in common with me. His predicted relationship with me was "nephew." *So I* do *have at least one secret sibling,* I thought. I sent a message in hopes that we could meet, or he could tell me what his parents were like, or he could get me in contact with his parents, or . . . I wasn't really sure what I hoped. But I messaged anyway, hoping at least for a response.

"This is [M]'s mom. His dad is [E]; both of his parents are deceased. But he is on Facebook." And there it was, some semblance of an answer.

M's mom had done a 23andMe for her son and herself, and she had no DNA in common with me. I had DNA in common with her son, so her son's father must be my sibling! Unfortunately, her son's father's parents were deceased. I had answers, but were they answers I could do anything with? I couldn't do anything about one of my parents being deceased, but I could at least reach out to E, who was M's dad, who was also my bio-brother.

"Okay will reach out to E. Thank you!"

"Looks like you are M's aunt! That's exciting. He doesn't have a relationship with E btw so that would be awkward, but he can talk to you."

"Thank you! Hoping it gets somewhere." I could've addressed the "aunt" thing, but I figured it wasn't the time quite yet.

Immediately, I pulled up Facebook on my computer and searched my new-to-me bio-brother's name. He went to the same undergrad as me! How fun. He also has a daughter. We've got some mutual friends: a poet, a person I used to go to church with, and a lady married into my adopted family. All three of them are folks I know from my hometown. And there it is: we share the same hometown! Everything is lining up.

Does he look like me? Maybe a slimmer, lighter, assigned-male-at-birth version of me. He's bald, so I can finally say that that runs in my family at HRT appointments. Nothing against bald folks, but I hope I don't become bald, only cause I'm unsure that I have the right head shape for it. His head is a peanut shape, though, so it looks good on him. He has a pretty smile. I'm unsure if it's the same smile as mine. Maybe a similar smile—am I looking too hard into things? I wonder why he and his son don't speak. I wonder why his son's mom speaks of him like they share nothing more than a child. Does men making children they don't take care of run in this family? I know it does in many.

He is . . . older than me; old enough to have three kids, at least. One daughter and two sons. The sons look like teenagers. One just did a basketball tournament; E looks happy for him in this picture. I wonder, if I send him a message, or a friend request, or both, what he'll say in response. Will he insist on calling me "sister"? Will he deny our relation, and continue living his life? I wonder what he might think once he realizes we are at least from the same city. I won't know until I try.

"Hey! This is KB, and I know I'm a stranger but I just got your contact info from M's mom. I just did a 23andMe test and got 23% of a match with M. I'm on there trying to find my birth dad, and I'd love any leads possible. Thanks for reading this 🙏."

Two weeks went by and I heard nothing from E. No traction on my friend request, and no "read" receipt on the message that I'd sent. I knew that messages from people you aren't friends with go to a separate folder on Facebook, so it was possible that he hadn't even noticed the new message. I check my message requests cause I sometimes get booking requests in there; there's no reason for someone not using Facebook for work to ever check it, I think. I wondered if the fact that we had three mutuals and hometown/alma mater similarities was enough for him to friend me. I wondered if it wasn't, and he just hadn't gotten around to declining my friend request. I wondered if he knew about me and decided to not get involved. He has a public profile, so I could see that he'd posted a couple times since I messaged and friend-requested him. He could be one of those people who post and log off, though. I know I am—at least with Facebook. I only have an account so my adopted family and bio-mom family know I'm still alive.

While I made up scenarios in my head, 23andMe notified me via email about a new message I'd received.

"Were you able to reach E? You are so closely related to M that you *have* to be E's sister. If not I have friends that still know him. Let me know if you need help." I pondered on this for a minute. If I could get in contact with E through one of his friends, why not try it? This option was offered to me, after all. On the flip side, though, if the man didn't want to speak to me, then was allowed not to speak to me. That would sting, but not more than not knowing a birth parent for twenty-six years of your life. I could handle it if that was his reality.

I still needed to address the whole "me being trans" thing with this lady, who up until now had been nice to me. Still, I knew that if we continued to speak, and she continued to refer to me as "aunt" or "sister" or something else of the *woman* variety, I would get bothered. It already makes me uncomfortable. *Why am I thinking so much about this—about everything?* Well, when have I *not* had to think about my transness in service of someone else's feelings? When have I not had to make up shit about a parent I never knew? Nobody who wasn't trans themselves has ever made me feel like I didn't have to "come out" to them. Still I pondered, until I conjured up a reply that felt something like right:

"Hey! I haven't heard back from E. It looks like he hasn't even seen the message. Bummer! If you have any other folks I could reach out to in the meantime, I would appreciate it!"

Immediately, M's mom responded, "This is an old email of his: [E]@hotmail.com. And the last phone number I had of his is ______. I'll ask if my friend will message him. It wouldn't hurt to try to reach out in another way." Again, I had to try.

And *try* I did, this time in hopes that it would lead somewhere instead of a perpetual "I don't know" when asked about my bio-dad—somewhere my question mark could be replaced with a period, a comma, a sentence I can reread until I tire of its known ending.

For twenty-four hours, I agonized over what I should say via email. This was my second chance to make a connection with my brother—a chance that was my only option outside of calling. Years ago, a therapist told me: *Do not initiate things if you're not sure that you would be mentally okay with the worst-case scenario happening.* I would not have been okay if E hung up in my face. I typed and untyped a comprehensive email about myself, my bio-mother (in case it rang any bells), and my reasons for reaching out, though I was unsure I needed to explain why I wanted to know my bio-father.

Do you know what it's like to not be able to put a face to characteristics you can't trace back to the one part of your bio-family that you know? Do you know what it's like to have eyes, ears, a smile that you can't name, to have a mother folks can't say "you look *just* like her" about? Do you know what it's like to have health risks from a DNA strand you think you'll never know, so you and your Black self must tell an almost-always-white doctor you don't know your dad, and they give you that "I'm sorry for you" look, E? At least, I hoped E had a relationship—hopefully a good relationship—with our father before he died.

Subject line: Hello + Trying to get in contact
Message: E,

Hey! This is KB; I got your info from M (your nephew?)'s mom, and I recently did a 23andMe test to look for one of my birth parents.

I was adopted in Fort Worth, TX in 1997; I now live in Austin—about 300 miles away. M's mom was saying that I may be closely related to you (like, sibling-level) based on my results. Will attach below for you to see.

[picture]

My legal name is "[deadname]" (hence why that's on me and [M]'s shared family tree). If you could at all give me any info on your parents, I would appreciate it! I'm just trying to pick up the pieces of possible relatives and thank you for reading.

Best,
KB

The rest of the month happened to me. I checked and re-checked my emails, and I gave my Facebook account more logins than I'd given it since 2010. I kept returning to an empty inbox, and emails I'd rather not check. I kept giving myself opportunities to be disappointed in men that I don't (and may never) know. It was a rainy lead-up to spring, and I felt more lonely than I'd ever been, wanting, gunning for the possibility that I'd know more about a dead man, that I would at least gain a new connection from the storm called KB that my bio-dad never got to know.

"I emailed him and no reply yet! Just wanted to update ya. Also I think that I sent an FB request but will check if I actually did," I said, faking the excitement I once had to M's mom.

"Ok I just emailed him too and sent him your number. We will be in Austin in June for a week and would love to get to meet you. Maybe we can go out to eat or cook out and you can show up and surprise M. He's never met anyone from that side and my family is mostly passed too. I'm [D] on FB. M is ______, but he doesn't get on there. His pics are really old."

M's mom had been so nice to me. Sharing E's name, email, number; suggesting I chat him up on Facebook. Even though nothing had come of it yet, she was genuinely trying to be helpful. I forgot that strangers could do this: be nice to me. It helped, maybe, that she wasn't a stranger to me anymore. We had one loved one in common; M was newly tethering us to each other. I could love M soon. I could play basketball with him (though I am no good at basketball), or eat BBQ with him and his mom at some spot I recommended in Austin. We could sit at a park and they could fill me in on what M's dad is like; M's mom could maybe even tell me what my bio-dad was like. I could see someone from that side of my question-mark family and see if any semblance of me had rubbed off from M's dad into M's face. If I got nothing else out of 23andMe, at least I'd found a nephew and his mom, a phrase where there was once a redacted story, an entry point to a closed-off section of questions that my heart had been suppressing for decades.

But before we met, I knew I had to tell her.

I'd had this conversation a million times before. The discrepancy between the name/gender on my driver's license, or birth certificate, or any other "official" documents, and the way that I appear—to the gender-ignorant eye—as *male,* or *undifferentiated* (fun fact: a year into my medical transition, two doctors put this on my medical records) has made me a pro in outing myself when necessary.

"I go by KB," I'd mutter before handing over a W-9. "This ID is old, but you can still see my face in it. I'm KB by the way," I'll say, half-assuredly, as I hand a bouncer my ID. I changed all my profiles. I picked usernames that include "KB." I filled out *Preferred Name* for any place that offered it. Since I was twenty-three, I've distanced myself from my first name. But I didn't change my profile name from my legal name before I messaged M, so they'd already seen that my name wasn't "my name." I guess I was too eager to inbox M. I didn't do my usual concealing.

23andMe, at the time, also required that you disclose your sex assigned at birth to DNA Relatives, so even though I'd already said "my name is KB," M's mom knew I was "female," and addressed me with the shorthands and pronouns folks automatically associate with that. I had to tell her that's not me. A familiar nervousness bubbled up inside.

It's important I note that my feelings of hesitancy aren't unfounded. All across the globe, trans people are retaliated against by their cis counterparts when they out themselves as trans. In the best-case scenario of dealing with a transphobe, you could see discomfort color their face and every action they take toward you going forward. It doesn't feel good to immediately know that your likeness has made someone feel fearful, confused, disgusted, or all these at once. That experience alone is enough to compel you to keep quiet. Other scenarios, however, include more heinous actions, like verbal or physical attacks.

A notable number of Black trans women in particular are killed when they disclose their transness. The simple act of saying "I'm trans" to the wrong person—and so many people, cause of worldwide anti-trans sentiments, are the wrong person—has consequences that could lead to death. This reality curdles in my veins every time I'm forced to out myself—IRL or digitally. There is no time, place, or situation where I've said "I'm trans" and knew that safety was waiting for me on the other side.

So I typed and untyped this message, keeping close my therapist's words about being prepared for the worst-case scenario. Would I be okay if M's mom was uncomfortable, fearful, or verbally violent toward me via 23andMe? I couldn't map out the possibility in my brain. I couldn't let myself see the emotional state that I'd be in afterward, since getting this close to an answer for who my bio-father was had never felt possible until now. Would I be okay if that was no longer possible, if I had something that I wanted—longer than I've known what "want" is—being snatched from me cause of something I cannot control? This wouldn't be the first nor last time someone didn't want to share space with me cause I was trans. I've gotten through worse things than someone saying mean things to me. Or had I gotten through them at all?

Does "outing myself to a relative of a relative on 23andMe, in hopes that I can learn things about my dead bio-dad" spell out *gotten through it* on a sheet of white paper? I don't know. The message I sent looked something like this:

"Hey! I for some reason can't see your last message, but I got it in an email. I wanted to let you know that I'm trans, and I go by the first name KB and use they/them pronouns. I hope that that is cool, but I wanted you to know before we planned anything!"

April. More than six months after my initial friend request, E finally acknowledged, but didn't accept, it. I can still see his profile, and I know sharing the same hometown and alma mater isn't enough to accept a person. Or we didn't have enough mutual friends. Or I didn't look familiar enough. Or my message popped up on his iPhone, or Android, or laptop, or desktop, and he chose not to open it; or thought it was too much; or he never saw it, and rejected my friend request just cause. He's allowed to do this. I always thought he was. At least I can see his profile. I shouldn't like anything or he'll block me.

It's been two weeks since I sent M's mom the message. She hasn't logged in for five days. 23andMe doesn't tell you when someone has read your message like Facebook does, and maybe she logged in super-quick five days ago to get a PDF of M's lineage.

He is 55% white. Maybe that means that M's mom is white. Maybe she hasn't seen my message from two weeks ago, or maybe she has and has blocked me. But you can't block people on 23andMe, I think. I close the app, get back to my life as-is, and mourn the sentence I'm unable to read.

Memorial Day comes and goes.

E never read my Facebook message, so I unsend it. I don't wanna be known to a stranger, uninterested in knowing me, as an illegitimate sister. Since you can't unsend messages on Gmail (unless you do it right after you send), I don't wanna be seen as a needy orphan. *Oh shit;* I realize I called M his nephew instead of his son! Maybe that's why he didn't reply.

I send a quick email saying "I'm sorry, your son M!" Maybe he'll know I meant no harm. I'd be mad if some stranger called my son my nephew, too. But me and E aren't strangers anymore. We are, in the sense that we've never spoken. We aren't, in the sense that we share at least 50% of the same DNA, but he does or doesn't know that yet.

I've been working super hard for myself all year, so I finally have five hundred dollars and thirtyish hours to change my first name on all my "official" documents. I close my laptop, and better my life as-is. I wonder how M and his mom spent their time in Austin.

The summertime happened, then fall and spring again. The closest person to helping me find closure about my bio-dad stopped replying to me when I outed myself. I cannot say I'm surprised—that the capacity for niceness stops at a cis person finding out that you are who you are—but I can say that I didn't plan on it, the silence being the worst-case scenario, the silence being the thing that was a crueler alternative to telling me exactly how she felt about trans people. At least when I've been heckled—on street corners, emails, or social media—and told that my rejection of gender is detestable, or told why I'll never be loved, there wasn't a landfill. I wasn't left with a silence on top of a silence that already existed, those silences doing a death dance in the hallowed places of my heart. I don't know if I ever stopped asking questions—from thirteen to twenty-six. From one adolescent lifetime to the next, I kept asking impossible questions of people who were always going to fail me. "Why didn't M's mom reply to me?" is too easy a question; "Why is the world like this to trans people?" is more applicable and possible to know.

If I could give you a dime for every time I looked in someone's eyes and saw something I couldn't see in myself; if I could give my untraceable eyes to another; if I could trace the genes that exist in me to something bigger than just me; if I wasn't so scared to pass on diseases that I can't name; if I could tell you who my bio-dad was; if I could turn back the hands of time; if you could tell me what the fuck is so wrong about a person listening to a body they don't know why they have, and a mind that doesn't know what it's made of, and tuning out a society that claims that listening to a body is a cardinal sin, or an illness, or a death sentence; if I wasn't so prone to being silenced; if I; eye; I; I—I wasn't so tired of looking and seeing—

The next April, I visited my adoptive parents out of the blue. I had planned to come to my hometown to see friends, but after years of avoiding the past, I felt up for seeing them.

"Hey!" I said, happily. I let their eyes wash over my face, which was more hairy and aged than the last time they saw it. My chest was also flatter, hairier, and exposed due to my typically two-buttoned shirt.

"Hey!" they said, somewhat surprised by what they were seeing. But mostly, I could tell, they were happy to see me. They opened the door for me to walk in, and we talked about my new name and pronouns.

I answered some of their questions, pushed back on some of their ignorance, and took bites of my mother's usual Sunday breakfast in between. We had a conversation that wasn't possible when I came out in high school. There was more understanding, more patience, less grief and loss in the air. I stayed until I wanted to leave; while I stood up, I said this:

"I'm so glad I got to see y'all today."

They agreed. My father walked me to the door.

four

"Sir?," "Ma'am?," and Other Things I Miss

1.

Black Kid enters a coffee shop, stage right. They sport a graphic tee with the words SUGAR, WE'RE GOING DOWN and black jeans with a studded belt. The fake studs are falling, only saved by an occasional push-in-place by the Black Kid, their eyes smeared with clumps masquerading as mascara. Their eyes are blurring out everything on the way to the counter. A barista stops talking to a coworker, her straight and stringy hair stuffed under a cap that says COLE'S COFFEE SHOP. She meets the now-anxious Black Kid's eyes to ask:

"What would you like to order?"

The Black Kid, wanting to try something new but loving the comfort of familiar things, whispers:

"A PSL with oat milk, please."

"What did you say," Cole's barista says confidently, and less confidently says, "ma'am?"

The silence rips between them like paper, loose-leaf and gone into the wind of a Texas fall morning. "Sir?" Cole's barista says, just as unsure and loud for everyone to hear, as before. The furrow in CB's brow—mixed with her searching, reaching for the right innocuous greeting, a *Southern hospitality,* a region's oxymoron—brings Black Kid's eyes to a new point, a random groove in the iPad register.

"A pumpkin spice latte with oat milk. Grande," Black Kid whispers, gently, back.

"Okay. Is there anything else?"

2.

It's odd to miss embarrassment. Especially when those
moments—still vivid down to the touch—
disconnected you from reality. Like any habit that once
served you something like comfort, or felt like a human saying
I love you without a corresponding *despite,* it's human nature to miss
the violence you've learned to put up with.
Sometimes I miss home and then I eat a sandwich.
Sometimes I want to call my cousin, tell her all her bullshit—
You shouldn't look like a boy and other misgivings—is forgiven,
but lies have never sealed up a wound. Home is a matter
of circumstance. You were born into a city who marked you
by time then marked you in other ways, didn't it? I am nothing great,
never been typecast as beautiful in any magazine, still haven't
figured out a way to love that isn't a vacant alleyway,
but I do miss other people's uncertainty. You know what I mean?

3.

Legally Black Woman enters a courtroom, stage left. Their head sags like a heavy load, exploding* under the pressure of a summons to jury duty. Everybody else in the room is white. Prosecution, judge, defendant's counsel, Greek chorus of people from all over the city who got the same letter as Legally Black Woman—all white. Except for them, and the defendant, who has the hue of half the state, speckles of brown, ~~dark enough for a dark cell~~ dark enough to be in this courtroom, with a stain of innocence over his face nobody

* This references Langston Hughes's poem "Harlem."

except me can see. His lawyer, a white man with circular glasses, the kind of white man that would be on the cover of *GQ*, says:

"Do you think that cops are more truthful than civilians?" Legally Black Woman squints their eyes at the word "civilians."

"Yes," says juror #38, a white man with bulging blue eyes.

"What about you, Mrs. Brookins? . . . Oh, I'm sorry, Mr. Brookins," he says, in a tone that soothes as much as it stings. In a tone that kind of sounds like Legally Black Woman's voice when they look in the mirror every morning before work. Legally Black Woman, now summoned to speak, sits in a chair, their burgeoning beard a mainstay in the mind of the lawyer who sees the *F* next to their name, and oscillates between the choice to ignore it or uphold it as Legally Black Woman speaks:

"No. I don't think they're any more truthful than a kid who will say anything to get candy from his mom's purse. Can I be dismissed?"

4.

Hello _____ how are you
Excuse me, _____
Dear _____, I need an extension
Nice to meet you, _____
I don't make the rules, _____. I just enforce them
Yes _____
No _____
_____ moiselle
I started to feel old when I was addressed as _____
Please _____ may I have some more
_____ Elton John
Good morning, _____
Please lower your voice, _____

Wham-bam-thank-you-_____
_____ upstairs; please let _____ rest
_____ Paul McCartney
You have the right to remain silent. Anything you say can and will be used against you in a court of law, _____

5.

Legally Black Man walks up to the stage. A woman who claims to have read all their poems approaches the mic to introduce them. They're wearing a homemade black crop top, which slightly exposes a pudge and love handles. Their jeans are ripped enough to teeter the line between straight and queer. Who's to say except a fifty-word bio. Their years-old sandals hold on to their lotioned feet for dear life. Tonight might be their last use. The woman—smile painted on both sides of her well-meaning face—says:

"Let's now welcome the man of the hour: LBM!"

The crowd erupts. Legally Black Man opts to change his naturally reflexed frown into a smile, so fake it could be sold at Hot Topic. They've made a life—some lines and a handful of good times—out of a number of misfortunes, so this is a walk in the park, right? Legally Black Man walks, with purpose only gathered from taking life with its lifelong failures, and sets the mic on fire. Once the fire department's been called and a number of expletives have been hurled, they say, to the crowd, calm and with careful purpose:

"Thank you. Are there any questions?"

6.

If we were in our last hours and
you had nothing but the sound of my voice
carrying you through the woods

created by bombs, a race war, a staged
panic brazen/raised only by the holders
of dollars and ways
they rationalize giving us pain, still
you would search for an honorific
to give me, a gift I didn't
ask for, a way to define and historicize my voice.
MY voice. My VOICE. my voice.
What devils we unearth when we speak
his name, what mind games we play
when we liven the legacy
of Christopher Columbus. What terrible things
we name in our moments of seeing—
when the light is so close to us, it flickers
on and we jump—the customs we can't trace
I want to give this name, this gender
to a flame and make it
eat my transgressions for dinner, make it
feel all the shame of confusion;
if curious was a viable option, I would take it,
but would you let me
could you let me
have you ever let me
be bigger than the boxes a form can hold,

braver than the thoughts a judge
will ever make, heavier than a barista
making common, global mistakes
I want to live in the gray matter
of earth, grow roots and be tall
Let my children speak truth and watch you

empty every bin, light every match,
set fire to everything so I have nothing to miss
While the coroner takes pleasure in warming me up,
asking what happened
and writing nothing down

Male Dis-Privilege

In April 2020, I started my medical transition. In the belly of a pandemic no non-politician or non-scientist could've predicted, and looking into a year when I couldn't find one reason to not take risks, I did the thing I'd been thinking about on-and-off since I knew it existed. What I've seen in the mirror since I was young—a genderless Black being who wants the outside world to see them that way—couldn't be actualized unless I had medical intervention. The things that tied me to womanhood were my voice, my chest, and my body shape, so I decided that—to live in the world more authentically in the gender-ignorant eye—those things had to change.

I couldn't have predicted what would happen next.

Within two years, I'd had top surgery and started HRT, meaning my boobs were gone, my upper body was stocked up with muscle, my voice was two octaves deeper, and I had hair—sprouting out and staying put—everywhere on my body. I had enough itchy stubble to feign the outline of a beard, and the things I was told would be cons (balding, acne, and aggression) had been minimal to none. Second puberty has been subtle, then gradual, and now constant. If then-KB saw me, they'd say that—besides the beard that still needs to come in—I've gotten everything I wanted out of a medical transition.

The social transition, though, is what gives me pain in different ways every day.

In April 2021, I was still doing way too much shit. By that I mean I was the executive director (ED) of two super-underfunded non-

Me in 2019 (pre-T) vs. 2023 (3 years on T)

profits, still working a full-time job in student affairs, trying to stay on a constant reading/writing/submitting-to-new-opportunities schedule, and preparing to start grad school in a couple months. I could see an end in sight, and had already told both nonprofits that we'd have a new ED by August 1. These were all things that felt exciting, but man, did it also drain the shit out of me.

At this time, my voice was in that "definitely lowering day-by-day but doing a weird squeak every time I speak too loudly" phase. Cause of this, plus a new flat chest, I was getting mistaken for a dude all the time in public. I figured this was just part of the process—being nonbinary and on HRT. I didn't think being mistaken as a Black man would be worlds different than people thinking I'm a Black lesbian.

At one of the nonprofits I ran, we had newly appointed a white woman to a managerial role. I was more or less happy about it, since me and this person had a fine rapport based on our minimal interactions, and she got the consensus vote. Before taking a much-needed break from that job to vacation for a week with some loved ones, I left a video detailing all the things that needed to get done during my week away, and some things we needed to cover at our next team meeting—one of them being that we all give suggestions for improvements to our team processes. I gave some examples of things I'd like to see improve, and then ended the video requesting that they bring any they had.

Harmless. Short. Sweet. Or at least I thought so, until our team meeting.

Apparently, this white woman spent that whole week internalizing every suggestion of improvement I'd given to a nine-person team. She also felt it necessary to defend herself, defend her team (they later expressed that they didn't ask her to do that), and shit on the whole organization unconstructively for twenty minutes on a Zoom call. Being overly familiar with the White Woman Meltdown—the passive aggression, the overt aggression, and the way they like to escalate things and take no accountability for their actions afterward—I responded with a request to speak more about her frustrations during a facilitated discussion later that week, since she'd made it glaringly obvious that her grievances were toward me specifically. She talked one other time on the call, and during that second, twenty-five-minute White Woman Meltdown (extended version) she complained that by shunning her for speaking earlier I wasn't being "equitable," and saying further negative things about the organization; all this was directed at me. She then avoided me—and all my requests for an amicable conversation—for two weeks, then quit the day we had our facilitated discussion scheduled. Before I blocked her from all the access she had to our organization's systems, she mentioned her therapist saying that it was "unhealthy" and "unsafe" to engage further with me specifically.

I've dealt with white bullshit before, unfortunately. But this felt *different.*

Past the obvious anti-Blackness in the ways she was acting (plus the weird "equity" comment), she also tried to convince a group of people that I was *dangerous.* Somehow, my light defense of her inaccurate accusations during the too-long Zoom call was read as aggressive, out-of-line, things said with the intent to belittle her team of non-Black people. The aftermath was irreversible damage.

At a time when we were already phasing me out, and working our asses off to fundraise for increased wages and more programming, people lost capacity for the work. Multiple folks were offended by her notions pointed at "the organization," and the team bond I had worked so hard to create withered. What was left was individuals creating ideas about me—some thinking I was terrible for *checks notes* not letting a white woman berate me based on shit she assumed in the first place.

On November 3, 2021, months after the White Woman Meltdown, I was an intern at a sexual health clinic known as the place for queer and trans people in Austin, Texas. As a Black, queer, transmasculine person eager to break into a new field of work, I was eager to work with them, especially cause I'd be serving mostly queer people of color. In a meeting with my new supervisor, she looked over an email I was about to send to a patient. It had "Hey hey!" as the initial greeting, a phrase I frequently say in-clinic. To my surprise, I was told that my style of communication was unprofessional.

By this time, I had at least eight years of experience watering down Blackness for non-Black people (no matter how "progressive" the space), so my response was direct and delicate. Though professionalism is anti-Blackness personified, I replied:

"I disagree, but okay. I will change it." Though we both had on masks, I could tell that her face was chock-full of shock. I naively thought that we could surely move past this moment. Reader, she proved me silly.

As I sat, eating some chips in a conference room at this sexual health clinic, a clinic I was happy to unpaid-intern at, I was perceived as disrespectful. So much so that the school supervising my internship was told I "rolled my eyes" and "was packing up as [my supervisor] was still talking." So much that I was called "combative" and "unregulated" for trying to make peace with this woman while maintaining my dignity. So much that me saying "this hurt my feelings" was heard as "I'm unable to take ownership"; me saying "I need" was heard as a demand.

When my new supervisor was faced with the music of her misreadings, and when she was told plainly by me that her behavior was anti-Black, she decided to badmouth me in my school reviews. Her "pro–queer and trans" superior did all but fire me afterward, so I turned to the sexual health clinic's HR in hopes that I could get some guidance about it.

"So I said how it made me feel in a meeting, and they both responded to me—"

"Well, they have a right to respond," said the white man who worked in HR.

"I know, and I didn't say they didn't. What I was going to say is . . ."

The call was peppered with defensiveness from HR. Shortly after, my supervisor was told—without my consent—that the call had happened and chose to resign from supervising me. I was also told to "work from home for the rest of the semester," and I wondered whether she had requested that we not share space. I didn't have a person—not even the one whose job it was to help—invested in saving me, so I had to leave. I had to take a lower grade than I earned, and leave the internship early. Weeks after this, I decided to leave the grad school program I was in.

Why couldn't *she* work from home, you ask? Why did I have to take a lower grade? Because Black. Because masculine. Because history.

In the U.S.A., Black men lead all the worst races. They are the highest demographic of people incarcerated in the states; they lead in unemployment, homelessness, and substance use prevalence when compared to men of other races. When it comes to sexual assault in particular, Black men are significantly more likely to be wrongfully convicted for it.

Black men lead races no one wants to win.

Volatile reactions to the presence of Black men is nothing new in the U.S.A., either; we have a hefty history of state-sanctioned brutality against Black men, the most glaring example being police brutality. According to Marc Mauer's "Addressing Racial Disparities in Incarceration," one in three Black men born in 2001 can expect to go to prison in their lifetime. The rate of Black men who are slain or battered during police interactions is ridiculously higher than for any other demographic. We also have the history of white women accusing Black men of being violent toward them; the Emmett Tills, the Central Park Fives, the Anthony Broadwaters—all the Black men who had their life (or parts of their life) extinguished for the perceived-mistake of being Black. I won't act like I know what it means to be currently or previously incarcerated, but I do know all too well what it means to be dangerous.

In instances of anti–Black masculinity (like the two instances I experienced), Black masculine people gain traumas that we must work through alone. In less than six months' time, as my skin got oilier and my body got hairier, I was accosted, lied on, discarded, and made to feel like I'm violent for defending my character on two different occasions. I've seen the change from when I was perceived as a butch Black woman to now, how the cutting eyes of invisibility and laughter turned into frightened stares. I can see how these constant happenings could lead Black men into unhealthy coping habits that harm everyone around them—domestic violence, sexual assault, and substance abuse, among other things.

I had negative interactions when I was Black butch; the only difference from then to now is that my emotions are now largely ignored. In 2018, scholar Shahan D. Bellamy highlighted the phenomenon of Black transmen and (hyper)(in)visibility. "Hypervisibility is an acknowledgment that these experiences are what makes up their personhood, and that their oppressions are always in conversation with each other," Bellamy said. Black transmasculine people live with the plague of Black masculinity (a threat in the non-Black gaze) and Black femininity (invisible in the non-Black gaze). Though I identify outside of the binary, this fits my experience all too well—the world denying your existence, and communities treating you as invisible, and then, as a monster.

Since 2021, I have had many other incidents where someone tells me—with or without words—that they're scared of me. As my body changed during the earlier days of my medical transition, I peeped the newly formed terror that non-Black people felt when they perceived me as a Black man. I went from "erasable masculine Black woman" to "hypervisible, scary Black man" in every space I dared to enter within twelve months. It didn't help that I'm big. It didn't help that I'm not overly friendly when it's not required of me. I thought it was just me, experiencing this violent re-socialization, but I've since talked with other Black men—cis and trans—about how they're been perceived over time. Those people, multiple Black people who were men too soon, who transitioned from a girlhood to a manhood they did or didn't want, validated that it wasn't just me. These days—due to Blackness and manhood mixed into one—people see me as *hostile* all the time. This isn't something I could've prepared for. I didn't have the (dis-)privilege of being a Black boy first.

How many Black men and masculine people do we have in the prison system simply cause they were around a non-Black person that deemed them unsafe? How many people can disappear until we don't have enough Black fathers, brothers, sisters, lovers, friends in this nation? How long can we live in a world where Black people need white people in order to right violent wrongs? When will we not be wronged?

These twistings of the truth, my truth, go untamed; this is not out of the ordinary for Black men and masculine people. I say "masculine people" cause this is not just a Black men's issue. Though this gender-ignorant world may see me as a Black man, I am a Black, queer, nonbinary person who embodies masculinity. I can't ask for a table, dish out an unassuming grin, give compliments, or disagree with someone without being seen as an enemy, as danger, as disappeared to the non-Black gaze. How do we disappear Black butches, Black studs, and Black masculinity in those we perceive as "women" from Black families? From the non-Black field of vision? How do we disappear Black men who do nothing wrong, besides exist? Black masculine people are aggressors before we are seen as human.

These harmful perceptions of Black masculinity are perceptions the world has made. Becoming a Black man in the United States is my forced and bitter privilege.

My first year of being perceived as a Black man was the hardest of my life, and not just due to unjust hostility. For Black trans men and Black transmasculine people, we've also got a thick layer of transphobia and black-and-white thinking to navigate. In feminist discourse, for example, cis women (correctly) claim that men have more job opportunities and pay. For the first two years of my medical transition, though, I didn't have the money or time to change my legal name or gender marker, so anytime I filled out a job app, I had to embarrassingly explain transness and gender to folks who could—upon learning I'm trans—decide not to hire me. In many states, including Texas (the one I live in), there is no law banning anti-LGBTQIA+ discrimination. I've only ever been "out" as trans in one workplace. My specific field is writing—in a state where taxpayer money is being spent to investigate and ban LGBTQIA-related books. I ask the question: "How will I get my words to people who need them without someone saying my existence causes them 'discomfort' more than I'd like to?"

I could miss out on money—the thing that keeps this country in business and keeps me housed/fed—for my Blackness *and* my transness. Is that a privilege?

When you live your whole life with the world thinking that you're a Black girl, and you decide to give up trying to fit into Black girlhood, and you become a man that you didn't ask to be, no one gives you an injection of "male privilege" juice. There is no packet that says YOU'RE A MAN! with balloons and stickers on it. All of a sudden, I couldn't give constructive criticism to a team of people I led, and I couldn't count on my "male privilege" to get me more job prospects. I also couldn't count on the medical field taking me more seriously, since the (useless) (painful) federal binary still identified me as *F.*

When I finally partook in my necessary medical transition, I didn't decide to get bottom surgery or a hysterectomy (not like the latter would've been easy), so I still have to get reproductive care. Black cis women are routinely dismissed and discriminated against in healthcare settings. That very much happens to Black trans men and masculine people, too, except it's also coupled with a lack of transgender care expertise. Couple medical anti-Blackness and misogyny with no way to designate your name—one you chose for yourself—on intake forms. And a majority of doctors/front-office staff not knowing how to use your pronouns. And a phone call with ten-plus security questions cause they're "just trying to make sure that you're the right person," since your insurance says *F.* And no private restroom without an *M* or *W* sign to make sure you don't get hate-crimed trying to pee. And a million other things that would bore you if I got into them fully. Getting your legal name and gender marker changed is expensive, and makes some things even more complicated (like getting care designated for "women") on the insurance side.

Is this a privilege? Am I gaining something with this new lost capacity?

I'm not saying that male privilege doesn't exist. I'm saying that the level of privilege you "gain" when going from being perceived as a "woman" to being perceived as a "man" is relative. Telling someone like me, who still gets she/her'd once every blue moon, that I have "male privilege" is wack, especially considering that I live in a Black, trans context. "Male privilege" is often reduced to some (white) (cis) feminist own—like "you'll never carry a baby" or "I am more oppressed than you"; often, in a trans context, "male privilege" is only somewhat recognizable in the experience of white trans dudes. Of course they gained that shit! They often have money and access to expedite their transition, and white men have been the pinnacle of maleness and beauty since this godforsaken country has existed. If your feminism is limited to "man = bad"/"woman = good" and you're not educated on the expansiveness of gender, you're not making progress. You're more making the type of social change we've always done: incremental bullshit that gets reversed, and that leaves out entire groups of people.

What we think of as male privilege is relative, in the sense that it depends on race, boobs or no boobs, vocal range, shape, and how you carry around your body. Most people, if they think I'm a dude, think I'm a gay Black dude cause I don't pantomime the limited body language that cis maleness exudes. Queerness troubles male privilege as well; ask any gay man ever. Male privilege is also, especially in trans communities, dependent on time, money, and access.

Getting your legal name and gender marker changed requires that you spend ridiculous amounts of time updating everything that has your legal name on it. Birth certificate, driver's licenses, credit cards, passports, Netflix logins, insurances—everything. Who has the time, money, and access to do that? Oftentimes, not people like me. Male privilege also depends on location and culture; what it means to be *a man* in America is different overseas, and I'm she/her'd more when I'm around other Black people.

My hope is that more people embrace the nuance and flexibility that exists in our lives. Male privilege is not black-and-white, just like race, sexual orientation, and all other man-made constructs. It's social, and social rules bend depending on many variables all the time. I wish that well-meaning, ill-informed feminists would stop being transphobic in their ideas around reproductive justice and misogyny. Including trans people in our organizing means that we are actually addressing everyone affected by the issues—bodily autonomy, reproductive rights, domestic violence, classism, etc.—and we've expanded the number of people that can organize against our actual enemies. After all, do cis women want to be seen as a vagina and boobs, or do they want to be seen as women (read: *people with rights*)? Why does their understanding of their own womanhood and the womanhood of others hinge on body parts? Your rights should not hinge on the oppression of others. Period.

Intercommunally, I hope we also learn that treating men like they're the devil reincarnated will not bring about change. Sure, it may feel cathartic, but the trans guys and transmascs catching strays from your inaccurate juxtapositions of "man" and "woman" don't deserve that. *We're in the 2020s! Some men don't have dicks!* Both of those sentences are objective. Also, I hope we stop having all-white-trans-guy panels. They're not reflective of the trans experience, therefore shouldn't exist. Learn to step back, white people!

I wake up every day with the worry that I will disappear. Whether it be by the hands of the police or someone sitting on a bench at a park, there is always that margin of possibility that I will look too much like a criminal, too much like danger, to someone. And I carry that with me in every interaction and phrase that I utter to a non-Black person. This is a worry that is unfairly dished to people like me. Even with self-correction, anti-Black masculine ideas that have nothing to do with me appear in the minds of people who interact with me. And then, I even question myself.

No matter where I am—queer/Black/trans-friendly or not—someone can decide that I am unsafe and have me disappeared, never to be heard from again. I have families—chosen and blood. In too many Black families in the states, there is a silence, tombstone, or a collect call where a man or masculine person should be. Do you feel that power in your hands? If it's not in your hands, do you feel it in the hands of others? Do you know, even if you've spoken with integrity and are a "good" privileged person, that you can do this to me? If not, do you know that others can do this to you?

We deserve better. Black masculine people deserve sovereignty and safety. We deserve to be seen as kind, to disagree with someone, to even mess up without having our lives taken, to not be seen as discardable. Black masculinity isn't synonymous with violence. Black men trying to exist next to you isn't a cause for concern, nor a right to disappear them based on the violence you *think* they possess. I don't need to be reprimanded for being alive.

I am not an enemy of feminism. I believe in a world where everyone—regardless of gender, sexual orientation, and all the other things that make us different from each other—has access to a good life. I hope you believe in that, too.

Texas: An Exodus

I travel the globe wondering where I'll be
the least haunted. Is it legal to be gay; can I get
hormones without insurance haggling me.
Is insurance needed; is it a barrier between me
& a good life.

Will the doctor gawk at my
vagina. Will the doctor ask am I a man or a woman.
Will I have to be a man or a woman; is there
a beach, places to rollerskate, places for the dog
I don't have yet. Are there trees—trails of leaves

me & my lover can walk & lie in is all I ask. I must travel
the globe doing a game of lesser evils.
A state is a state of mind & this body
has had enough. I'm breaking up
with what I've known—these lonesome stars now shining

full-grown. These people I've come to call home
in times Abbott & Patrick have tried to call me
home. These pavements made for driving
& crying alone. Even this
dystopian land gives me much to miss.

The bliss only given by Texas BBQ & sun
beaming the same on any shade of skin. I can't know
what would pull me back if I stay here,

battered; let another legislative session shatter
my insides like crab legs I happily crack in this heat.

I'm put in the predicament of missing
what I can't find elsewhere
on this planet: something not actively
trying to end me/somewhere
that won't tell me be grateful & pledge

to what aims to destroy you. I've got to believe in something
else. I want to fly into a life I don't have to leave
bruised. I travel into a state, wondering what
state doesn't pride itself on borders,
& every face isn't colored with an aftershade of red.

A Trip to the Gynecologist

I was twenty-six. Twenty-six years past the doctors saying "It's a girl!" when I came into this world. Five years past the recommended age of first receiving a Pap smear. One year past starting HRT. Six months into what many believe to be the "peak reproductive years" for someone with a uterus.

I was twenty-six, living in the middle of the shit show that is Texas politics, and the number of laws that criminalize me being Black, trans, and able to give birth are mounting up higher than my five-foot, nine-inch frame. I'm making the brave choice to live in a time when many people in power would rather me not. I hadn't gotten a Pap smear in years due to a lack of health insurance, time, or the spoons to go through with the process. Maybe I want kids someday. So I went to the gynecologist to know my options.

Before doing the thing that most cisgender women do—simply calling a clinic or practice—I sprinkled my browser history with searches. On Google: "trans-friendly gynecology in Austin, Texas." On Facebook: "Who knows a trans-friendly gynecologist?" On Instagram, addressed to my close friends: "Does anyone know any trans-friendly gynecologists in Austin?" I continued searching for an hour. I didn't have more time than that.

Based on my years of experience with doctors, it's safe to assume that most medical offices don't know a damn thing about trans people. They don't know any greeting that's not "sir" or "ma'am"; they don't know how to use any non-he-or-she pronoun. They don't have a field for you to fill out a name that is not your legal name, and they will equate two genders with two body parts every time. I've found this to be true of gynecologists, primary care physicians, sexual health workers—all of them. Unless it's a clinic specifically catering to trans people, I don't expect them to know anything. I expect resistance to me correcting them, since I'm not the one in the conversation with a medical degree, and elitism has the medical field by the throat. Some trans folks I know expect even more violence. It was 2021, and I was trying to see a gynecologist.

Finally, I came across a couple of Facebook comments that mentioned an "LGBT-friendly" practice. I typed, "When you say LGBT-friendly, what exactly does that mean?" into Google; Google doesn't have a good answer. I knew then that I had to call the clinic myself.

There's this thing that happens where "LGBT-friendly" means "LGB-compliant" and nothing else. Often, it means the practice has one white gay man on staff, so they think all their internal inclusion work is done. Like, "*RuPaul's Drag Race* quotes are on the walls and rainbow confetti comes out of their mouths as they mis-pronoun me" type of places. I'll be pointed to the women's room when I need to pee, then hear "sorry, it's a reflex" in these places. Before I leave, a "yes, girl" will slip, followed by an "I call everybody 'girl'—even my male friends!" in these places. I called the clinic that was recommended to me.

"Hello?"

"Hey, this is KB. I'm calling to see if y'all take BCBS and have available appointments next week."

"Yes to both! Are you calling for somebody else?" the person on the other end of the line asks.

Pause.

Over the past six months, my voice had dropped something like two octaves, so the "ma'ams" I used to get had become "sirs." This person was likely assuming that I was somebody's husband, or son, or friend calling in place of the typical womanly voice that needs a gynecology appointment. It would be fine if it wasn't the tenth time this week that a stranger had mistaken me for something I'm not based on my voice, or face, or something else we shouldn't use to determine people's gender. So I answer:

"No. It is for me."

"Okay, what is your name?"

If I could choose a phrase to explain how I feel much of the time, it would probably be *trans fatigue.* "What is your name?" can be a surprisingly complicated question depending on your class, or race (since white supremacists from 1619 to present have made class and race almost the same thing), or age, or if you feel any affinity for a name somebody else chose. For me, "What is your name?" is a question that elicits a quick pushing of my ID across a table, in hopes that they can read it and not ask me again. Since this is over the phone, I had to explain. And explain again in a couple of minutes. And misname myself, then explain again to more people every day until I found the five hundred dollars I needed to legally change my name to something else. Trans fatigue is the everyday fatigue of being trans in an embarrassingly cisgender world.

"My legal name is ____________, but I go by KB."

"Should we put 'KB' down as a preferred name?" I'm asked.

"It's not really 'preferred.' It is what I want on anything that doesn't necessitate my legal name. Is that okay?"

"I have to ask my manager."

This is a conversation I could have in my sleep. I had it with my friends after debuting my new name. I had it with every job, and new friend, and family member that I thought wouldn't be violent when given my new name. I had it with myself—but not with cashiers or baristas. I don't have the energy to correct strangers during brief interactions, so I am whatever they call me that day.

"Okay. Will I have to use the restroom at all as part of my visit?" I ask.

"We may need a urine sample."

"Do you have gendered bathrooms?"

"What do you mean?"

In 2016, Texas (along with almost every other state in the South) attempted to pass a law that restricted transgender people from using restrooms that coincide with their gender identity. Cause of some scienceless, needing-a-distraction-ass lawmakers in North Carolina, every trans person who hadn't had their legal gender marker changed was about to be subjected to violence and embarrassment if they needed to use a restroom outside of their house.

It is as silly as it sounds, and cause I'm nonbinary, restrooms labeled "men" and "women" don't feel useful or comfortable for me to use. I've heard enough passive-aggressive "they're letting men use the women's restroom now" comments while peeing in a stall that has a sign featuring a faceless blob in a skirt to last a lifetime. Hearing the F-word from scary-ass strangers while leaving a men's restroom feels like the norm at this point, so I'd rather take a leak anywhere without a sign on the outside of it, or with a sign that says GENDER NEUTRAL.

I mean gendered, unlike the fucking bathrooms in everyone's house, is what I wanted to say back to the person, but they're a stranger. Instead I said, "Ones with men and women signs on them."

"I think the restrooms inside our facilities don't have signs on them."

I let out a sigh of relief. Eventually we finished this predictable conversation and I had an appointment scheduled for a few weeks later. Are you as exhausted as me?

—

I got to the clinic fifteen minutes early, as requested. I was greeted by the receptionist—and a bunch of stares. If you ever want to know what people look like when they see someone they think shouldn't be somewhere, be my guest at the ob-gyn. I'm sure the white ladies clutching their purses (since my transness comes with Blackness) would love it.

"Hey! Are you here to pick something up?" the receptionist asked me.

"Nah. I'm here for an appointment. KB at eight-twenty."

"Oh, okay! I'm sorry. Take this with you and bring it back when you've filled it out."

All the things that Black girls deal with in medical settings are doubled when someone is uncomfortable with your presence, your nonconformity to their ideas of gender.

If you're leading the crusade against men, I'm sorry to burst your bubble; I get hell too, and I'm not a man, just forced to be one by a binary world. When I'm in the doctor's office, they treat my ass the way they treated me when they thought I was a Black girl, plus worse. When I say anything about pain, or pleasure, or fertility, or disagree with anything a provider says, I might as well have cussed them out. Their insistence on being the "expert" gets in the way of care I need. I've been made an expert on transgender care due to the gaps in knowledge I've encountered from professionals, and because of my desire to learn so I can advocate for myself cause there is no one else equipped or willing to do so. There is no magic wand or alternate universe that saves me from womanness. A gynecologist isn't so different.

"Hey [deadname]!"

"It's KB."

"Oh yeah, that's right. So sorry about that. What are you needing today?"

I wish I could've said *Understanding.* I wish I could've said *Someone I don't have to explain my humanity to. Someone with a more-than-101 understanding of what it means to be trans. Or what it means to be trans and Black and filled with fatigue. Someone wanting to be competent and humanlike to both demographics. Someone I trust to hug me.*

Instead I say, "I want to know if I can have kids."

Texas abortion providers are still fighting an anti-abortion bill that became law. There are still many, many media outlets greenlighting unintelligent, reductive, unhelpful, and inaccurate pieces that defend using bio-essentialist language* when talking about reproductive justice. There is such a lack of research and competence around trans men and transmasculine people that providers who actually are trans-competent can't tell me whether taking testosterone impacts my number of eggs. Yet wanting people to use accurate language like "pregnant people" or "birthing people" instead of the limiting and inaccurate term "women" has so many trans-exclusionary and ignorant "feminists" (you can't possibly be radical or a feminist if you think this way) rising to the top of a boiling-over pot.

It's not cute, nor is it new, to make the assertion that people like me don't have a right to be included in conversations that impact their own experiences and hopes. No matter if the gender-ignorant

* For example, calling abortion a "women's rights" issue even though it also affects trans men/trans nonbinary people.

gaze makes a split-second decision about my reproductive parts based on what I look like; I can still become pregnant. I still have a vagina, uterus, fallopian tubes, and scar flesh where boobs used to be. All the shit that a cisgender woman gets for needing reproductive services, I get, plus about two more hours of work—not to mention embarrassment and trans fatigue.

If abortion rights are built on "pussy power" and some kind of sameness attributed to everyone that is identified as a woman, then we will continue to fail. If abortion rights are withheld from some—as they have been from Black women and trans people since their inception—then the movement will continue to fail. Reproductive justice means the right to bodily autonomy for all who are directly impacted by sexist, ignorant policies that attempt to tell people who can get pregnant that they can or should be forced to have babies. If being asked to change "women" to "pregnant people"—or to take a fucking workshop on gender and sex to start unlearning all the toxic shit you learned in K–12—makes you foam at the mouth, we will never have justice. Instead we will only get small, incremental bullshit "progress" fueled by outrage and money that ultimately only helps a few. We saw that with the "women's right to vote" movement and how it conveniently excluded Black women. Why are we cool with leaving people out, again and again?

I'm not being doom-and-gloom; I'm being realistic. Anti-Blackness and transphobia are cooked into almost every mainstream conversation of reproductive justice, and that's a problem. The sooner we name our missteps out loud, stop patting ourselves on the back for caring about cisgender women only, and cease the creation of "woman and nonbinary" spaces based on ignorance in the guise of inclusion, the sooner we get to anything that is closer to justice. Before I even enter a reproductive space, I am invisibilized. I want you to know that men aren't the only demographic to blame, just like not all women menstruate.

At the end of the day, bodies are just bodies. That's true in Texas, across all these other divided states, and anywhere that has silly little markers for gender and sex. *M and F* is bullshit, just like any conversation that refuses trans and Black inclusivity. Reproductive justice means every person that can have kids can have them when and if they want to. It also means I can make a call, set an appointment, and leave with all the answers I need.

Black and trans people deserve better. If you want me to say more, you'll have to pay me.

Red

I'm twisting myself in a pretzel trying to speak to you
I'm wringing language of all it has to offer
in order to feed you this life

This possibility of Black kids never knowing what fear is
This apex of Native kids knowing exactly what is home
This religion, empty of condemnations
This surplus of earth and her resources
This vexed interest in making the quiet part—
our dignity—loud
I could say more but they'd call me a terrorist

To admit that this isn't working,
to say what I see isn't perfect, but I want us all to see
that once I get to the bottom of Naima,
to the interests of John Coltrane,
his need-to-know basis, his painting
of a new world through hands and sound
I will crown all of us: important

I can't begin to tell you how much
I wish I could paint a picture
The conflict, our inter/intra conflict
that doesn't call for anything resembling a gun

I wish I could make you believe in us
and move past a plane, this plane

that makes us feen
for what we need to survive
If our baseline wasn't in a deficit,
we would still have unanswered questions
but which would you rather answer
Will I die today in the hands
of a global pandemic,
or the headline: courtroom ~~gone wrong~~
gone American,
or see more accidental pregnancies,
see more rights folded up in favor of greed—

This country is a dichotomy
leaving little room for the best of anything
disabled, poor, or racialized,
do I want to figure out my red

in the comfort of arms
and hearts
who don't want to see me dead
I don't believe in lies. But I believe in us.
Doesn't that count for something?

We Are Not Untouchable

I published a piece of writing for the first time in 2015. Ecstatic, still learning the ins and outs of what poems could do for me and my people, I heard that my undergrad's student-run literary journal was accepting work for their upcoming issue.

The idea of seeing my words somewhere outside of a YouTube link intrigued me. At this time, I had only known poetry through the spoken word group at my high school and many of the poets I watched on Button Poetry—Danez Smith, Franny Choi, and the like. Many of them had secured book deals, were starting MFAs, making a career turn from the stage to the page, and getting millions of eyes on their work in the process.

I wanted this: Something to make my words feel real. Something that told me I could make a life out of writing poems. Something that taught me how to make money from stanzas; after all, we all are artists living in a country run by capitalism. After submitting to the undergrad lit journal twice, one of my poems was accepted. With that small confidence boost, I submitted to a couple MFA programs hoping that I would become the capital-P poet I saw on my laptop screen.

I thought the MFA was like a place to find my community. Since I didn't have one at my undergrad, and I had no knowledge of community spaces that would give me the knowledge I thought I needed, surely this was the place I'd get friends and answers to all my questions. I got into two of the four MFA programs I applied to, and it felt like a sign that all the claps and awards and happiness were an arm-stretch away.

And then reality set in.

The MFA I attended was ridiculously white. I mean, "ask you to explain Blackness" white. I mean, "I'm the only Black person in all three years of the program, and when I'm micro-aggressed the teacher checks on the other person" white. It was white as in violent as hell. I had never been in classrooms so tense and prescriptive, and that's not what I expected for a terminal degree in something as subjective as poetry. "Show, don't tell," they said. "To make this poem stronger, explain more to the reader or axe this line," they said, even though we spent most of our time deciphering poetry collections rife with jargon and the type of clunky syntax I only ever read in textbooks. It didn't help that there was no post-MFA path taught at this MFA except 1) get a PhD, 2) be a teacher, though the field is highly competitive, 3) be an editor, but only in the free time you have between being a teacher and getting a PhD. None of those paths felt right for me. We had no classes on submitting poems, submitting a manuscript, booking a show, getting an agent, connecting our words to social justice or any kind of deeper meaning. I didn't learn any of the shit needed to actually be a writer outside of the page. The type of writer I wanted to be—unapologetically Black, queer, and gender-confused; touring America; making the outcomes for kids like me better—wasn't taught in that program, and the more I questioned why it wasn't more helpful, the more I was pushed away by the academic engine.

Though I could've stayed and got the Blackness (and queerness) (and transness—though I didn't know it was transness at the time) beaten out of my words, I took the road less traveled and voluntarily left. Even if that program didn't work out, surely something would get me to where I needed to go, right?

Right?

The hottest summer I've ever survived was probably summer 2018. Texas felt like it was melting, and being in a perpetual state of confusion on what to do next with my life didn't help. With a layer of wet dirt and a dream, I packed up all my shit and moved to Austin, Texas, with a gang of other lost queers. I didn't have a job, so I spent hours on social media and at open mics soaking up everything that everyone said about what being a poet was like. I also spent a lot of time trying to figure out my gender and sexuality (since I'd finally moved away from the judgy eyes of my at-home friends and family).

"We are the truth-tellers," writers with checkmarks and an ounce of influence said on Twitter. If you scrolled through their comments enough, it felt like everyone agreed that writers were moral beings put on earth to wave their magic wands around to make art—aka be ambiguous and pretty. As I was learning more language about who I was and what I desired, I was also peeking into this literary world that made it seem like writers were beautiful.

Who doesn't want to be beautiful, especially after all the turmoil the academy inflicts on Black/queer/trans people?

After a couple months and Google searches, I landed on "nonbinary" as the closest thing to how my gender felt. "Why that line-break?" and "Why this inflection of voice?" felt like bigger questions than "Why have boobs?" and "If I was mistaken for anything, would I want it to be a girl or a boy" at the time, so I pushed medical transition thoughts out of my head. I put all my writerly questions into Google and compartmentalized everything else. After many non-answers and dead ends on poetry career stuff, I knew that I needed to find a literary space for folks severely underrepresented in the canon (like me) who needed a space to learn amongst friends. The classroom, after all, is a community space if you make it. Unfortunately, those spaces come few and far between, so I had to make one.

This is it, right?

This is the part where the awards, and financial stability, and progress for my people, and happiness for myself come in, yes? This is it, the moment I've been waiting on, right?

2019 was a terrible year. I was trying so hard to *prove* something—to show myself and others that I *could* be a non-MFA writer. I probably submitted poems once a week. On top of that, I was the host/sole organizer of a new artist showcase/open mic that was giving everybody everything but me. Friends told me I was "thriving," but I was actually suffering mentally. It takes a lot out of you—scraping up the little money you have to submit to contests and journals when over 70 percent of them tell you "unfortunately, your work was not accepted at this time." It takes even more to be the person that gives other people a community that you can't even enjoy; how can you commune at the open mic while also moving chairs, checking on performers, getting money to pay people, etc.? Some places I submitted to never got back to me at all. It was a rough time, to say the absolute least.

Often, marginalized people are tasked with creating their own spaces without the money, time, education, and other necessary resources to make them successful long-term. I was also, directly or not, asked to be the Token Black Writer or the Token Queer/Enby Writer all the time. My writing interests have never aligned with making my experience palatable to the white gaze, so I suffered. This type of suffering is often specific to Black, queer, and trans people like myself.

What happened to the magical writer? The one who did the right thing, and spoke truth to power when nobody else would? Where were those writers when I was wondering how I could get closer to my dream of being a Magical Poet™? The checkmarks who edited at the most-revered publishing houses and magazines didn't give me the time of day, and all the prosperity was going to the (consciously or unconsciously) token writers. I didn't know what to do next.

During the hellscape that was 2020, I focused mostly on my personal transition and working full-time. The long-put-off decisions of getting top surgery and starting HRT saved me during the most emotionally taxing year of my whole life. I also took 2020 as a break from the constant cycle of rejection and bad business practices in poetry publishing. Most acceptances were solicitations that I'm super grateful for receiving, and any fellowship I did was good timing and boredom. I somehow found myself writing prose during my fallow season of poeting, so I had a new reason to get out of my "fuck trad publishing" slump.

When I started participating again—this time in poetry and prose—literary entities proved true what I had known in my body since 2015: we, participants in literary America, are not in any way untouchable.

From "Who Is the Bad Art Friend?"* and "'Cat Person' and Me"† to the disrespectful discourse that shows its ugly head on Twitter week after week, so many writers' true colors shine. The true colors tell me that writers are not anything special when it comes to Having Morals or Being Humans. As I presented more like a "Black man" to the gender-ignorant eye, the literary scene appeared to be more volatile toward me. I tried so hard to get essays into my favor-

* The title of a piece published in *The New York Times* on October 5, 2021 (updated June 15, 2023), that went viral for weeks.

† The title of an article published in *Slate* on July 8, 2021, that also went viral for weeks.

ite magazines, and a number of times my opinions on masculinity and Blackness were invalidated by often-white, often-cishet culture editors and white queers at LGBTQ magazines. I could assume that it was transphobia and anti-Blackness stewing together to make something terrible, but the being-too-scared-to-be-wrong thing is too present in poetry and prose for me to ignore.

Often, it feels like the obvious points ("women are people," "save the planet from climate change") are revered, while intercommunal conversations—like how Black men need to do better, or how marginalization doesn't prevent someone from being harmful—are deemed unworthy of having. Conversations that pertain to reproductive justice, masculinity, transness, and Blackness are almost always missing a Black transmasculine perspective. There is a reason for this, and we can't chalk it up to human error or needing a "blind selection process" (which is ableist and doesn't stop anyone from being biased, by the way) anymore. There are no people like me at the editorial meetings.

To add insult to injury, many poetry-publishing entities charge people fees just to submit. For issues and contests, a $3 or $5 or $25 price of admission has become commonplace, even though most people with working fingers to google anything know that financial barriers = inequitable outcomes. Cause this (lazy) (wack) practice of charging people to have their work read has become normalized, the price of admission has only increased over time. It's hard to feel motivated to participate in a canon that wants so badly to both advocate for justice and price marginalized people out at the same time. You can't have both.

The truth is that there could be so many more people like me getting writing we need published and celebrated if literary America actually welcomed them. Who I am shouldn't need a news angle to be worthy of publishing. The plights I face trying to exist in America are not "too niche" or "incongruous to the experience of being a Black man." People straight up forget that folks like me exist—and that doesn't change, no matter how politically left the space is.

It's hard as well to not want to delete all my social media, since the same ideas from 2015 still fly and go viral. "Art is truth-telling" and "Poets are the good ones," they say, but my personhood has been dampened by the literary ecosystem continuously. I want to be able to talk about it, the dishonesty and binaries that we impose but say we resist, but I am often met with tired editors claiming they're "doing the best that they can." Why can't we decide, as a supposed community, to do something different? Something that doesn't always ostracize people like me?

It's time to be honest about the ways presses, magazines, journals, colleges/universities, community spaces, and all other participants in traditional literary publishing move, and if we—people in the literary ecosystem—actually want justice and to amplify voices, then inequitable practices need to end. Homogenous editorial boards, underfunded literary spaces, relying on hopeful writers to fund staff positions and operations—all this needs to end. We also need people and entities with influence, access, and money to stop hoarding influence, access, and money. Being quiet and greedy in moments when solidarity and support are needed is antithetical to what writing is supposed to do. There is no reason why creative writing programs should leave the business of writing to writing students to figure out; telling writers that writing is all it takes to be a Pulitzer Prize winner or whatever is not true.

We're not starting a movement when we put pen to paper, but we could be. That takes honesty, organizing, activism, and less wanting so badly to be morally superior to others. We can't keep lying to ourselves and saying that we are better than anyone when news, history, and everything else have proven otherwise. What do we gain when we lie to each other and the page? What do we lose when we think of ourselves as untouchable, or continue inequitable practices in the name of palatable production and faux-acceptance of Black/queer/trans poetics? I should be able to put "nigga" in a poem and not sift through journals to find one with a Black editor. I should be able to get all the things that my non-trans, non-Black, non-queer counterparts get, but I can't if it's paywall and "request a waiver" everywhere. Who has time to do that for every single submission? Who wins when we keep operating in this scarcity/individual-minded way?

Each adverse experience and day of literary discourse on Twitter should be radicalizing us to create a new literary America. Will that take people being more creative with the ways we write, create, and live with others? Will it take embracing the totality of people's personhood inside AND outside the page? I think so, and I believe it's possible if we address and solve the huge problems of the present. Writing is an extension of living, so we have to study and practice love in the same ways that we study and practice craft. We are not untouchable by the ills and devils of our society—which also means that we can be touched.

ACKNOWLEDGMENTS

Excerpts of this book appeared—often in earlier drafts—in *Spectrum South, HuffPost, Oxford American, Sundress Publications,* and *The Offing.* The poem "How to Identify Yourself with a Wound (2018)" was also published in my chapbook *How to Identify Yourself with a Wound.* The last line of "Sonnet Five" was written by Isha Camara, and is part of a crown of sonnets produced at Tin House (many thanks to my 2023 workshop with Megan Fernandes). I owe endless thanks to the many people who made this book possible. They are as follows:

Annie DeWitt, my sweet and fearless agent. I owe you so much for your advocacy and belief in me.

Erroll McDonald. You are the only editor who could've helped me get this book to where it was going.

The PEN America Emerging Voices program, for making creative nonfiction feel possible for me.

Belinda Yong, Brian Etling, Kelley Shi, Matthew Sciarappa, Nora Reichard, Claire Leonard, and all the other amazing staff at Knopf who helped bring this book to life.

The people that have taught me craft and cultivated in me a love of creative writing—especially Elaine Duran, Mrs. B Williams, Kiley Bense, Roger Reeves, Alex Lemon, and Curt Rode.

Leslie Shipman, for what you've built, and for introducing me to Annie.

All the characters of this book.

Gaby, for being my always-love.

My woes—Jazz Bell, Mah-Ro Khan, Davidra Patterson, and Kale Garcia. Our friendship has kept me afloat, forreal.

One more time for Jazz Bell. You make it so I can actually focus on words every now and then. I can't ever thank you enough.

All my mentors and matriarchs—especially both my moms, my grandmother, Dr. Stacie McCormick, and many, many others. I breathe and create because of you! I am blessed to have been raised by Black women whose patience and direction have kept me going.

My therapists, all of you that I've had over time—big ups, and sorry for some of the breakups.

The Anderson Center at Tower View, for giving me the time and isolation needed to finish this book.

To those whom I'm not calling out by name: charge to my head and not my heart. You know that you mean something to me, and that is what ultimately matters.

Thanks, lastly, to you for reading and being. May you stay as long as you can.

NOTES

ON MY HOMETOWN

38 **Multiple folks were arrested:** Andy Towle, "Gays in Texas Arrested for Public Intoxication in Stonewall-Style Raid," *Towleroad,* June 29, 2009, https://www.towleroad.com/2009/06/gays-in-texas-arrested-for-public-intoxication-in-stonewallstyle-raid/.

38 **The club burned down:** "Fort Worth Gay Bar Subject of 2009 Raid Destroyed by Fire," AP News, June 1, 2017, https://apnews.com/0a2e4e82e1484288a17ee63127b02fde.

44 **Gay marriage didn't stop:** Nur Ibrahim, "Is This a Real Interview with Dad of Colorado Springs Shooting Suspect?," *Snopes,* November 30, 2022, https://www.snopes.com/fact-check/alleged-colorado-springs-shooter-dad/.

44 **"Don't say, don't tell" repeals:** "Stonewall Riots," History.com Editors, *History.com,* https://www.history.com/topics/gay-rights/the-stonewall-riots.

45 **Joe Biden will still tell:** Laura Meckler, "Biden Administration Says Schools May Bar Trans Athletes from Competitive Teams," *The Washington Post,* April 6, 2023, https://www.washingtonpost.com/education/2023/04/06/trans-athletes-school-sports-title-ix/.

45 **Religious fundamentalism:** Moira Donegan, "Homophobic Businesses in the US Have a Powerful Ally: The US Supreme Court," *The Guardian,* June 30, 2023, https://www.theguardian.com/global/commentisfree/2023/jun/30/homophobic-businesses-ally-us-supreme-court.

45 **Transness is forty-nine lawmakers:** "2023 Anti-Trans Bills Tracker," https://translegislation.com/.

45 **"mutilating children":** "Debunking the Myths About Gender-Affirming Care," National Association for Social Workers, https://www.socialworkers.org/LinkClick.aspx?fileticket=SfQYdWPJAoY%3D&portalid=0#:~:text=MYTH%3A%20Gender%2Daffirming%20hormones%2C,provider%20supervision%20and%20clinical%20management.

OUR ALLEGIANCE TO QUEERPHOBIA

84 **Black women were asked:** Gigi Fong, "Not Dating Someone Because They're Bisexual Is Biphobic, Here's Why," *hypebae,* April 20, 2022, https://hypebae.com/2022/4/lgbtq-bisexual-dating-men-twitter-debate.

84 **In a 2005 study:** Elijah G. Ward, "Homophobia, Hypermasculinity and the US Black Church," *Culture, Health & Sexuality* 7, no. 5, September–October, 2005, https://www.jstor.org/stable/4005477.

85 **"varies from society to society":** "Gender and Health,"

World Health Organization, https://www.who.int/health-topics/gender#tab=tab_1.

86 **"So when Black people today":** Daniel Reynolds, "Why Can't We Talk About Homophobia in the Black Community?," *The Advocate,* May 26, 2015, https://www.advocate.com/politics/2015/05/26/why-cant-we-talk-about-homophobia-black-community.

PRETTY

115 **cissies:** Username @h3xed, "Cissy," June 27, 2023, *Urban Dictionary,* https://www.urbandictionary.com/define.php?term=Cissy.

MALE DIS-PRIVILEGE

180 **one in three Black men:** Marc Mauer, "Addressing Racial Disparities in Incarceration," *The Prison Journal* 91, no. 3 (2001): 87S–101S.10.1177/0032885511415227.

180 **The rate of Black men:** Curtis Bunn, "Report: Black People Are Still Killed by Police at a Higher Rate Than Other Groups," NBC News, March 3, 2022, https://www.nbcnews.com/news/nbcblk/report-black-people-are-still-killed-police-higher-rate-groups-rcna17169.

181 **"Hypervisibility is an acknowledgment":** Shahan D. Bellamy, "Diversity Scholar Candidate Discusses Intersectionality," *The Ithacan,* March 2, 2018, theithacan.org/28932/news/diversity-scholar-candidate-discusses-intersectionality/.

183 **a state where taxpayer money:** Nicole Chavez, "A Texas Lawmaker Is Investigating 850 Books on Race and Gender That Could Cause 'Discomfort' to Students," CNN, October 29, 2021, https://

www.cnn.com/2021/10/28/us/texas-school-books-race-gender-investigation/index.html.

184 **When I finally partook:** Mason Dunn, "A Person's Right to Choose," WBUR, June 6, 2019, https://www.wbur.org/cognoscenti/2019/06/06/transgender-reproductive-health-mason-dunn.

184 **Black cis women are:** "How Discrimination Can Harm Black Women's Health," School of Public Health, Harvard University—In the News, 2018, https://www.hsph.harvard.edu/news/hsph-in-the-news/discrimination-black-womens-health/.

WE ARE NOT UNTOUCHABLE

205 **the price of admission:** Emily Stoddard, "Submission Fees as of April 16, 2021," EmilyStoddard.com, https://emilystoddard.com/poetry-publishing-2021.